# BUILD IT BOLDLY

*How Daring Business Leaders Can Gain Influence and Create Impact*

## KIMBERLY McGLONN, PhD

Build It Boldly
*How Daring Business Leaders Can Gain Influence and Create Impact*
by Kimberly McGlonn

1. BUS025000 **BUSINESS & ECONOMICS /** Entrepreneurship
2. BUS070090 **BUSINESS & ECONOMICS /**
Industries / Fashion & Textile Industry
3. BUS071000 **BUSINESS & ECONOMICS /** Leadership

ISBN: (paperback): 979-8-88636-050-9
ISBN: (ebook): 979-8-88636-048-6

Library of Congress Control Number: 2024918969

Cover design by Nick Vicente and Lewis Agrell

Printed in the United States of America

Authority Publishing
13389 Folsom Blvd #300-256
Folsom, CA 95630
800-877-1097
www.AuthorityPublishing.com

*To everyone I've had the opportunity to teach, to lead, to be led by, or to watch achieve from afar, thank you for being the inspiration for* Build It Boldly.

*Having an idea and turning it into a business is very much like surfing a wave in the open ocean. Attempting to translate that journey into something helpful to others is a work of alchemy. Thank you to Marilyn Anthony for encouraging me to take this next step and for being beside me from beginning to end.*

*I want to thank my mothers, the circle of courageous women who have lovingly nurtured me in the various chapters of my life. Your tenderness, expressions of affection, and encouragement continue to be invaluable.*

*I also want to thank my father for the persistent push he gives me to keep going. You are my first and favorite coach.*

*I need to thank each of my sisters. You have always offered me words of affirmation and walked with me no matter the size of the mountain I was facing.*

*I'd like to thank my brothers for never letting me forget who I am and what I'm worthy of.*

*Lastly, I wish to thank my Noor, my light, my daughter. You are my life's masterpiece. You are a most incredible blessing and I am so proud to be your mother.*

*This work is dedicated to the memory of my Grammy, Ms. Barbara McIver Lucas.*

# CONTENTS

# INTRODUCTION

"What they gon' do?" is one of Victor McGlonn's favorite expressions. Victor says this often, but he also lives it. Never one to back down from a fight, he loves to push a boundary. He jaywalks, he dances and claps in store aisles when a song he loves plays, he jumps in the shorter line even when waiting in the longer line might be more appropriate. He has never been a man to ask permission, never a man to edit his language, or to back down from a fight. Instead, his default is to do what he wants, accepting that there may be consequences, open to potential conflicts. It's not that he doesn't see the boundary or the rule or the expectation. He just doesn't hold himself to them. It's not that he's inherently defiant or confrontational, either. He just knows that going the way everyone else has gone, waiting the way they seem comfortable waiting, surrendering to dominant structures the way dominant culture says he should, just isn't his way. He's a true victor, someone whose internal compass has always led him to act with courage, and sometimes recklessness. His internal defaults give him the spirit of an entrepreneur.

Victor is my dad and his "What they gon' do?" attitude has influenced almost every facet of my worldview and positioned me to take unusual leaps, from traveling alone in East Africa to resigning from an incredible position as a career educator to leap into leading cutting-edge companies. His motto has inspired me to not only empower the members of my professional teams, but to fully own my life. It's an attitude that's liberated me from submitting to the societal ceilings of racism, sexism, and poverty. My dad's default philosophy turned out to shape everything about who I was as a girl, who I am as a woman, and every major risk I've taken.

Perhaps Victor's spirit of "What they gon' do?" resonates with you, too. Maybe you, too, have always found yourself curious about unusual possibilities and now find yourself ready for an unusual set of leaps. It could be that you find yourself ready to challenge yourself, curious about your own potential. I imagine you recognize that you've become much more … *conscious.* You may not know the science or the full history of anything, but you can see that there are seriously alarming issues facing our country and our planet. You want to get involved, but on your own terms and you dream of creating a legacy you can be truly proud of. Perhaps you already have an exciting idea or passion for a potential product or service. Perhaps you quietly dream of growing that product or service, that passion, into a six- or even seven-figure company. Regardless, I suspect that you want your life's work to be a part of a bigger set of solutions and because of your focus, you're looking for a community of voices that will push you to ask, "What they gon' do?" at each stage of your journey.

You're not alone. I believe this is something many of us want.

## Building an Inspirational, Aspirational, and Profitable Business

I've been invited to share what I've learned to be true in schools of business and design all across the country, to speak to the entire federal Environmental Protection Agency (EPA), to sit on panels with other award-winning business leaders, and to moderate conversations with leading industry experts, in large part because what I've learned is so rarely taught. This is precisely why I've set out to share the most valuable lessons here. *Build It Boldly* is a priceless guide into how you can most efficiently:

- Give your business concept (regardless of its size) the frameworks it needs to make your community and the world more just, responsible, and environmentally conscious
- Employ the key understandings in creating the sauce you need for the inception and growth of the business, from a strategic planning perspective
- Become a locally, regionally, and nationally recognized social entrepreneur—one that people can't forget
- Absorb valuable creative direction and support in embracing the challenges of building an inspirational, aspirational, and **profitable** business
- Grow into a more daring leader, one not only able to see and understand, but use your very human story to create a positive impact

If you're ready to go after *that*, I want to push you to become what you're capable of being: an incomparable industry leader no matter your sector. Picking up this book is about your growth and also your own sense of personal purpose.

I've learned so much along the road to building the first Black-owned B-Corp (a business that has been verified by B Lab as meeting high standards for social and environmental performance, accountability, and transparency) in North America in the fashion space, one which went on to become nationally recognized and award-winning. It's been a climb that led me to open and operate several brick-and-mortar retail locations, a climb that sometimes felt like hiking up a mountain of gravel. This book seeks to share what that required of my teams and it will also make plain what it took me years to learn. And here's what I know for sure: the mindsets, principles, and strategies I've pursued must be shared with entrepreneurs, innovators, and business leaders like **you**. In my view, these lessons must be shared and adopted if the common good is to be protected and if we are to collectively survive whatever the climate catastrophe may bring. So, I've written this guide for you with vulnerability and transparency. After having faced both triumph and defeat, I'm ready to share some of the mistakes I made and the struggles I faced, in hopes of showing you how I went about shifting culture and provoked transformative conversations through several very intentional design choices. My experiences (both in life and in my professional careers) have undeniably shaped the person and visionary I've become. The things I've had to accept and the things I've empowered myself to choose have given me a compass for how to build bold, nationally recognized brands (yes, plural). And now it's your turn to lean in and to learn the codes, the very language of influence, and to step into even more focused leadership. They say once a teacher, always a teacher, and I believe that's true- this is why I'm offering this wisdom to you. May it give you the inspiration and strategies you need to risk defeat as you work to build something bold and transformative—something that aligns uniquely with your full potential. This, I'm convinced, is a most worthwhile effort.

# CHAPTER ONE
## Where We Start the Story Matters

"We cannot always choose whether or not we suffer, but we can choose whether or not our suffering will have been in vain."

—Marianne Williamson

There are two undeniable forces that shape all of our lives: the choices others made for us and the ones we make for ourselves. My parents, Victor and Charlene, could never have predicted what eventually happened to our family, but they somehow nevertheless prepared me from a young age to stand alone. In the longer view of their lives, they inherited a legacy of fighting—for freedom, for equality, for justice. That said, where we start our stories matters. I choose to trace mine, at least in part, back to my grandparents, folks who fled the American South as part of the Great Migration. My father's family escaped the terrorism that pulsated out in the open across the Southern states post the Emancipation Proclamation, and were successful in some ways at least. As refugees his people traveled north in search of reprieve from the violent, persistent racism culturally normalized in places like Pensacola, Florida and Fairchild, Mississippi, where slaveholding ensured generational wealth. His people settled near the shores of Lake Michigan in Milwaukee, Wisconsin. My great-grandparents were American migrants navigating a segregated landscape in so many ways, passing along recipes and laughing and dancing through it all. They were war veterans and sports hunters and laborers, and some, like my grandfather, were college graduates. They were courageous, driven, and beautifully imperfect dreamers. I am descended from these brave American folk who moved north, a mixture of genes sourced from Africa, Europe, and the Americas, folk determined to make a way.

When my paternal grandparents arrived in Milwaukee in the 1930s and 1940s, it was hardly the promised land they imagined. By 1960, Black folks made up nearly ten percent of the city's population. Restricted to living on the North Side due to widespread and government endorsed housing discrimination, more than sixty-seven percent of the city's Black families lived in unstable—and in some cases, untenable—housing. As was the case for many places in the country, Milwaukee public schools forced students to attend schools near where they lived, so housing discrimination invariably led to segregated schools. But this was met with resistance from both African American parents and educators and their White allies, who launched a decades-long campaign to desegregate the city's schools. Because of their activism, Milwaukee public schools were ordered by federal courts to integrate in 1976. I was born three years later. Over the next decade the poverty rate in the city nearly doubled, leaving four times more Blacks than Whites living below the poverty line. The proportion of metropolitan Milwaukee Blacks living in high-poverty neighborhoods rose from 8.4 percent in 1970 to 46.7 percent in 1990. By 1990, metro Milwaukee had the highest proportion of Blacks living in extreme-poverty neighborhoods of any metropolitan area in the fourteen Frostbelt cities.[1]

That was the backdrop of my childhood, but it doesn't capture the uniqueness of my experience. Despite all this exhaustion, all this depression, and all of this economic tumult felt by many in the Black community, my parents somehow arrived solidly in the middle class. During the 1980s, they both managed to secure highly sought-after union jobs with the United States Postal Service. Milwaukee has a little bit of a reputation as a blue-collar town where unions thrived at that time, and it was partly the power of the unions that pulled my parents out of the traps of poverty. Even though I couldn't have appreciated this as a child, it surely explains why I have always believed in the necessity of unions—without them, corporations have too much control and human rights suffer. This is important, often overlooked American history.

Despite these challenges, when I was five years old my parents saved enough to qualify for a loan for a handsome single-family house on Grant Boulevard. The North Side of Milwaukee was predominantly characterized by under-resourced, neglected blocks, but that block was among the exceptions. Being able to own a home on Grant Boulevard in the Sherman Park neighborhood was something all of my relatives admired and aspired to. Even now, nearly thirty years later, the details I loved about that home come back to me easily.

Our home sat on a bit of a hill, up one set of stairs, which led to a wide landing. Then, up a second set of stairs you reached the front door. The white-hexagon-tiled entryway led to a walnut-wood-paneled sitting room. A rust-orange shag

---

[1]    *A report created in 1988 by the University of Wisconsin-Milwaukee Center for Economic Development.*

carpet covered the long living room floor. It was, after all, the early '80s and shag carpeting was still having a moment. In our formal dining room, polished wood cabinetry ran the length of the space, with handcrafted glass panel doors reaching from wall to wall. Ornate white plaster decorated the ceiling with frescoes of carved fruits and flowers, and a hissing radiator encased in fine-grained wood gave us warmth during the dead of the long Milwaukee winters. Swinging wooden doors ushered you into the sunny kitchen, where windows revealed the blackberry and lilac bushes sheltered against one side of the house. We had the added luxury of a first-floor bathroom flooded with natural light from a window with a view of the backyard gardens. We also had the magic of our own home library. My parents kept their large collection of books, many by Black authors and about Black culture from around the world, behind the built-in glass doors. Our home library also held the full set of *Encyclopedia Britannica*, a prize I won during a public speaking competition at the mall. But their book collection was both impressive in its number of titles and in its diversity—my parents were voracious readers, insatiably curious, and they wanted their children to be, too.

Upstairs were four bedrooms, one for my parents, one each for myself and my two sisters, and a fourth room that doubled as a guestroom. Our house afforded us each ample personal space, and demonstrated the influence of the Frank Lloyd Wright architectural style, modified for the convenience and comfort of family living. We even had a laundry chute on the second floor that sent clothes hurling down to the basement laundry room. The chute was actually big enough to fit a small child. I never took the ride, but a couple of my more adventurous cousins did. And in the basement was a wooden sauna—not that it was ever functional while we lived there, but it existed—a relic of the families before. The basement also housed my dad's punching bag, which hung from the ceiling, and his workout equipment.

My bedroom was toward the very back of the house and looked out on a busy main street that ran through the North Side. It was painted 80s blush-pink, a color I got to pick out for myself. From the back porch on the second floor, we looked out over a symphony of fruit trees: sour cherry, crab apple, and pear, as well as the vegetable garden my dad tended to nearly year-round. It was in that backyard that I learned the smell of lilac blooming in spring, the tastes of fresh-picked blackberries and sour cherries. My father was an avid gardener and loved to cook and bake the way his grandmother taught him, using seasonal foods at the peak of flavor and using far too much sugar. But the legacy of recipes he inherited filled our home with warmth and kept our meals interesting. To this day, he is one of the most creative (and best) home dessert cooks I know.

I guess you could say that the house on Grant Boulevard imprinted me with the look and feel of the ideal family and home. We watched the popular TV sitcom *The Cosby Show*, which established a cultural narrative about the possibility of a Black doctor's family, and where most of the action took place in their Brooklyn, New York brownstone. And despite the fact that we were in the Midwest, my sisters and I totally identified with them. To this day, I love Phylicia Rashad, the energy of Brooklyn, and exceptional design, because they are all a part of the backdrop of my childhood.

However, as a child I wasn't aware of the stresses and strains my parents carried under the financial burden of purchasing and maintaining the home we had. In that way they did what many responsible parents try to do at least: they made me consider the cost of things, but never placed the weight of that reality upon me. In fact, it was only many years later that I learned my Uncle Bobby in South Philadelphia was the one who actually paid for our first Christmas on Grant Boulevard. He wired money to his baby sister Charlene, my mom, so that my parents could afford to buy us presents for a magical first holiday in our new home. That's how house poor they were for a time. My Uncle Bobby was the real Santa that year.

It wasn't just our welcoming house that made life so colorful and beautiful. Our neighborhood was pretty remarkable, too. Nestled between two major streets, North Avenue and Center Street, ours was an intentionally integrated neighborhood, home to mid-level managers, university professors, and middle-class families from several communities. We were Black, White, and a few of us belonged to indigenous nations. Thirty-Eighth Street Public Elementary School, where I started first grade, immersed me in this community. My school friends were kids from all sorts of families. Thirty-Eighth Street was one of Milwaukee's first test sites for meaningful school integration. My rainbow coalition of classmates included Anne, my best friend who was White, and Kate, my next best friend, who was Mexican American, and Adria, who was half Native American. I was a "walker," which meant my dad accompanied me the six-block distance from our house to school each morning and from school to home each afternoon. All through my early school years I was part of an exuberant, unself-conscious collection of high-energy kids with the great fortune of having teachers who encouraged and supported us.

My classmates' parents, like mine, were committed to integration, so we kids spent lots of time together. We slept over at each other's homes, played together both in and out of school, and we celebrated birthdays together. I remember my first taste of Potawatomi tacos at Denise's house—delicious, straight-from-the-hot-fat fry bread, topped with chopped lettuce, juicy tomatoes, and spicy ground beef for her birthday lunch. While we ate, her male relatives lined the street out front, straddling their Harleys, listening to rock music, and tossing back tacos. I had no clue how unusual it was in the '80s for a young Black girl to spend so much time hanging out with people who weren't Black. Because of my friend group, I was able to attend a Catholic mass and to be exposed to traditions I would have otherwise never known or appreciated.

At 38th Street Elementary my dedicated, fully present teachers showed me that teachers have the power to make us better versions of ourselves. I remember Mr. Hansen with his Paul Bunyan aesthetic and wardrobe of flannel shirts, but most importantly I remember the note he sent home with my report card. "Kimberly" he wrote, "is the epitome of what every teacher wants in a student." "Epitome" was not a word I'd ever heard, and I remember looking it up in the paper dictionary and feeling so special, seen, and celebrated. I cherished that note. In my opinion Mr. Hansen was the epitome of the teacher every child wants and deserves. But he wasn't the only exceptional teacher I had the privilege of learning from. In third grade I was fortunate to be in Mrs. Tucker's class. Mrs. Tucker was the only Black teacher in our elementary school. She ran a really tight ship, which meant she demanded daily excellence. Her faith in my potential produced what she expected: excellence. She rewarded performance, even taking me once to Chuck E. Cheese because I scored so unusually high on the state standardized tests for third-graders. Teachers are magic-makers. When you're Black and your teachers look like you, there's a special spell that can be cast. I grew in the rich classroom medium that she so generously tended.

These first years of school set me up to love learning and to admire and respect teachers. My default thinking has always been that teachers are remarkable, so you don't have to make a big leap to understand why I became a teacher. In some way, it was to acknowledge and repay the gifts my early teachers so freely gave me.

The thrill and fun of elementary school came to an end when I started middle school, and things only got much, much worse by the time I entered high school. The teachers can't take all of the blame. Society was changing—not for the better, as integration became contentious, and rapidly escalating White flight exposed how isolated and ignored Milwaukee's Black community would become and remain.

At the end of elementary school, however, a significant change happened rapidly in my family. Prompted by my mother's desire to belong to a spiritual community, we joined the Islamic masjid on the North Side. She set a new compass to move all of us in this direction. We went from no sense of having a large Black community to having a warm and lively one. Although we went to the masjid on Fridays for prayer and Sundays for religious school, these visits always seemed more social than mysterious or spiritual, at least in my child's eyes. And the Saturday fish fries were so culturally Black that it was like spending the day with your huge, extended family, something we hadn't had in our lives in quite the same way before.

My parents didn't give their young daughters a choice about accompanying them to the mosque, or wearing a head-scarf, but they did give us the strange and wonderful freedom to choose our new names, a very common practice for Black Muslims (i.e. Cassius Clay, Lou Alcindor, etc.). They made room for us to be whoever we wanted to be, and they did not try to influence our selection in any way. Being able to name my identity empowered and involved me in that new personality. Names are so powerful. Maybe even predictive of the future. Names are the stories of us that we choose or reject. When someone gives you a nickname, it's a way of owning you. When you take your own name, it can be a way of announcing who you are or who you want to become.

After carefully leafing through the huge book of Islamic names my parents gave us, I decided on "Amatullah," or "one who serves God or is a servant of the light." Even at age eight, I had a desire to be a servant, to be of good use. There's no doubt a willingness, more like a responsibility to be of use, was a value absorbed from my parents' generosity and goodness. That aspiration to serve became my true north. Meanwhile, at school I was Kimberly, Kim, Kimmy, or, to my bestie Anne, KimmyKimKim. Around the mosque I became Amatullah, or Ami for short. I'm sure I didn't reflect on it in this way at the time, but living this duality of bouncing in between identities didn't mean behaving differently for me. Throughout my life, I continue to be known by many names. It never created identity confusion for me. If anything, there's a richness and complexity about being known in different ways by very different people that just proves how complicated life is. I was a girl who became a woman at ease with being a multi-hyphenate, with being many things at once.

When they weren't spending time at the masjid, their jobs at the post office allowed my parents to have inverse schedules so that one of them was always available for kid care—Mom worked third shift and Dad worked evenings. The schedule played to their strengths. Dad, the easygoing guy who could talk to anyone, took me to school and went on many of our class field trips. He also was the better cook who happily made our dinner most nights. Mom took me shopping and thrifting, two things she deeply enjoyed. And while I often found the shopping tiresome, she used these excursions to encourage me to find my own style. My friend Anne remembers me as "always styling," though my "look" in the '80s was hardly mainstream. Layering was what I remember doing most, dressing for school with a base layer of long johns (it was Milwaukee, remember) overlaid with a turtleneck and bubblegum-pink leather pants, pulled together with a chunky belt. My mother taught me to wear whatever I wanted, with only the occasional intervention, and mostly when she thought she was protecting my modesty.

Mom was an accomplished seamstress, using the skills she learned from her mother, a union garment worker in Philadelphia when the city was still a textile manufacturing center. My mother didn't make my everyday clothes, but special-occasion outfits were a different thing altogether. They were our shared collaboration, starting with a trip to the fabric store. One such occasion was my fifth-grade graduation. For the occasion we traveled together to JOANN Fabric on Milwaukee's South Side. This cavernous space held hundreds of blocks and bolts of fabrics on shelves that stretched from floor to very high ceilings. Those top tiers were way too high to reach. If you wanted to inspect a bolt of cloth from the top, one of the staff wheeled over a ladder with a platform, climbed to the ladder landing, then grabbed the bulky length of cloth with a tong-like grabber tool. But before choosing fabric, we had to select a dress style. Set just inside the store entrance were the circular towers of wire racks displaying the McCall's pattern packets. Row after row of racks filled with eye-catching paper packages featuring color photographs of smiling models, all of them White, posing in dresses, slacks, blouses, jackets, and coats of various cuts and styles for every occasion. We'd slowly spin the racks, my mom and I, pausing at some, quickly whirring past others. Finally, we agreed on a pattern for a drop-waist, mid-calf dress, long-sleeved with a bit of ruching at the shoulders—a dreamy but modest look suitable for a ten-year-old Muslim girl.

Next came the choice of fabric. We scanned the walls of fabric, taking in the plaids, the messy florals, the shiny satins. My mom taught me the difference between charmeuse and georgette, the difference in drape and feel. And she taught me that the look has to fit the occasion. I think I understood that because I was her oldest child, what we were celebrating with my graduation was a bigger occasion for her than for me. From all the overwhelming options available, I just wanted to find something pretty. Peach satin, with its suggestion of optimism and gentility, spoke to me. I was, after all, a modest little Muslim girl with a headscarf. Mom supported my selection of fabric and color but thought sparkles would be a nice addition—a sparkly, lacy overlay on the bodice. I didn't like sparkles then and to this day I don't like sparkles. I guess my aversion can be traced back to this graduation dress. I remember my mom preparing to make my dress. The way she pulled out the leaves of the dining room table so she could unfold the life-size crinkly paper dress pattern she'd bought. Then, she would ease her heavy home sewing machine out of its box and sit down to the meticulous work of measuring, cutting, stitching. If you've never made an item of clothing, you'd be surprised by the Frankenstein-like wobbly, wonky process of it all. Each piece of a dress is made separately, held up or tried on to fit the arm or the back or check the skirt length. Then, the pieces get stitched together to form the finished dress. My mom worked on this while I was in school, so in my daily absence it seemed to come together magically.

On graduation day, I slipped the dress on and stood in front of the mirror, admiring the new Payless slip-on flat shoes we had dyed the exact same shade of soft peach. Mom had used a bit of extra fabric to fashion a headscarf that I wore over my hair with the help of a lot of hairpins. I truly hated the sparkles, and I can still feel the stiff itchiness of the satin, the way it scratched my skin, the way it ruched where the lace met the satin fabric at the hemline. My ten-year-old self felt a mixture of discomfort over wearing something handmade instead of store bought, but also took great comfort from the loving care my mother had put into this dress.

This dress held so many of her emotions. It was a symbol that she'd created especially for me to display her pride in my graduation. And, as it turned out, this was a momentous day: it was the first time I was asked to speak in public all on my own. I remember moving really carefully to the center of the school's gymnasium because I didn't want my headscarf to come off. Even though I can't remember even a bit of what I said, it became a defining moment for me. I went on to get involved in public speaking from the sixth grade on, though thankfully never again having to wear sparkles or being trapped in stiff, shiny satin.

A penchant for stylish dressing and artful décor must be an ancestral affinity. My great-grandmother established herself early as a fashion icon for me. My cousins spoke proudly of her all-white living room, where everything was carefully sheathed in protective plastic that crinkled when sat on. In summer, their bare legs stuck to the coverings. Great-grandmother Sadie Harris wasn't designing for comfort, but for impact. Everything about her house and the tailored way she dressed spoke to careful presentation and thoughtful arrangement. Nothing out of place, nothing left to chance. And never anything mismatched. Her taste perfectly captured the '50s and '60s style, and she never got caught up in any passing trends. I grew up appreciating her mid-century style that, like her, seemed timeless. This attention to detail also showed up in her garments—they were always well tailored and full of delicate details. Fashion always tells a bigger story than the surface reveals.

My maternal grandma Barbara, Sadie's daughter, was another style influence. She was always on trend, enthusiastically embracing every new fashion wave. Her beautiful style earned her a nickname she still recalls with pride. "I was the Black Liz Taylor of South Philly. They all called me 'Black Liz.'" Until she was ninety-five "Black Liz" continued to express her opinions of current fashion trends. A visit with her always included a clever quip about whatever I was wearing. She was regal and relentlessly rewarded elegance.

After my fifth-grade graduation, I moved on to the Lincoln Middle School for the Performing Arts. I threw myself into all the opportunities for artistic expressions Lincoln had to offer. As a theater major with a dance minor, performing around the city in various plays and recitals like *Hansel and Gretel* and *James and the Giant Peach* became part of my learning world. Encouraged by my initial exposure to public speaking, I competed in forensics, which is a "speaking sport" where students participate in public-speaking competitions. I entered a school-wide competition, reciting a long poem I had committed to memory about Harriet Tubman, the heroine who helped enslaved Blacks escape the South via the Underground Railroad. Although I no longer remember the poem, I remember how deeply it moved me and how hard I practiced being able to convey my emotion in my recitation. My performance by eighth grade was good enough to qualify me for the state competition.

The weekend of the state competition, my dad proudly drove me the three hours it took to reach the auditorium. He watched from the audience as his Black, Muslim daughter, the only one in a headscarf, proclaimed her poem from the vast stage. My efforts won me third place. On the drive home, Dad was angry and upset. "You were the best in the room, no doubt," he began, "but what you were delivering, they just weren't ready to hear it." He was so sad. "You were cheated, Ami, and that's just the truth."

That day showed me so much about who my dad was. As even younger children, my sisters and I would begrudgingly go along when Dad coaxed us to accompany him to the boxing gym. Hours spent with him at the boxing gym provided a drastic contrast to my dreamy hours at the library. At the gym we sat ringside, inhaling the steamy, salty air. We watched my dad training young male boxers. He took pride in mentoring them with their boxing, but also by helping them transition to adulthood. At the gym, Dad's pleasure as a coach and a role model animated him. His joy was impossible to miss. His instruction wasn't limited to training young men, though. Eventually he'd turn his attention to us, teaching us how to make a proper fist, poke out a jab, and land a solid punch on the speed bag. Our reward for doing our best in this smelly place was his encouraging praise, reliably followed by a post-workout frosty cone from Kopp's Custards. That day affirmed what in many ways I always knew. I had an amazing father.

My dad's belief that his girls needed to be able to defend themselves was not without justification. While my elementary school years were safe and secure, by middle school things were different. I was the only Muslim girl in the school, and my headscarf became a ready target. Quickly, I learned to walk the halls with my hand pressed against my hairline to protect my scarf. Even then, I rarely made it through the day without some boy, thinking it was funny, yanking my scarf off. It may seem like a small act of aggression, but it was terribly humiliating to be exposed in such a personal way. All the other girls had neatly combed and styled hair. Mine, tightly bound under my headscarf, was the ultimate bad-hair-day look. By exposing my "scarf head" hair, it made me look unkempt and lesser. That ongoing exposure was my first experience with public shaming. It never occurred to me to complain to my teachers. Years later, though, when I became a teacher, it made me much more sensitive to any form of ostracism my students underwent, and intolerant of the bullying that too often accompanies being seen as different.

When Dad wasn't teaching us self-defense or immersing us in nature at local parks or in his lush background garden, he was teaching us about Black history and African history. Had I been raised by different parents, maybe they would have discouraged this side of me. But Victor and Charlene, both Marquette University students, recognized and encouraged my fascination with stories. In fact, now I realize that for the most part, I always did what I wanted to do with their solid support. My father was a talented boxer who wanted to teach me to defend myself.

Both he and my mother bought us games and books from the local Black-owned bookstore, but beyond that, they made a point of engaging with us. They asked us questions that made us think. They shared ideas that added to our insights. They made sure we saw successful people who looked like us and who my parents admired. Our dad was affectionate, funny, and relentlessly nurturing. This was expressed in his food, his affection, and in the ways he spoke to us in equal prose and poetry. During these crucial formative years of my early selfhood, he was fully present, every single day. Undeniably, his approach to parenting shaped me in ways I am still only beginning to see and understand.

Growing up on Milwaukee's North Side gave me many beautiful moments—memories of walking through the gardens of the Domes and of Milwaukee parks in the '80s, when Washington, Sherman, and Lake Shore Drive were thriving public spaces. Dad would cajole my sisters and me to jog along with him, or to go for long hikes or bike rides. He made sure we spent a lot of time outside learning to breathe, to observe, to appreciate the beauty and wonder of the planet. His presence was a major anchor of my incredible fortune. But the backdrop of Milwaukee in the 1980s and early 1990s was also really generous to us. That city, in that neighborhood, at that moment gave us small mountains of fresh snow to eat and throw at each other in the winter. Our zip code gave us diverse friendships, sleepovers full of craft projects, and countless roller-skating sessions. It afforded us the Wisconsin State Fair, Summerfest, and opportunities to celebrate Juneteenth Day on MLK Drive with friends who were more like family.

At the same time, the focal point of my own compass was just coming into view.

But what I hold onto most from my days in that complicated city, was that my life there was colorful and wonderful. Even though my family enjoyed the luxury of vacations at Disney World, Grant Boulevard had been the happiest place I'd ever known. These are some of the many pieces that made up our home on Grant Boulevard, some of the earliest grace-giving and character-defining choices that were made for me. This solid, loving foundation proved to be what separated me from so many of my peers, something I could clearly see by the time I reached ninth grade, the parents I once knew had begun to disappear.

## Key Takeaways:

- **None of us get to make all the choices that shape our lives. When the choice is yours, build on what is positive in your past and will help propel you forward.**
- **You decide when your story begins.**
- **Teaching is magic-making. What are you teaching others in the way you show up?**

# CHAPTER TWO
## Somewhere on the North Side

My earliest significant trip without my parents was to a Muslim youth conference in Chicago. I was in the seventh grade and the prospect of even a short road trip without them was intimidating. But nothing catastrophic happened on that journey, so my parents felt comfortable sending me on my first Black Achievers college tour that same year. It was important to them that I learn to be comfortable on my own in the world, and excursions like these were safe but powerful first steps.

My young, adventurous spirit found Black Achievers group travel experiences to be well- everything! I was in some ways completely free, and the campuses we visited seemed worlds apart from the North Side. I'd already been to Chicago and New York City, though I had to forge my parents' signatures on a check from their bank account to pay for that one. The risk was worth it. What these places represented—the unknown, the independence, and the freedom in an academic culture—was practically irresistible. Not only that, but they offered me a chance to step into one of my other favorite television shows: *A Different World*. They gave me a chance to see the trendy fashion and feel the energy of HBCUs (Historically Black Colleges and Universities).

When I was in the eighth grade, I joined a group of about twenty-five other teens to go on the Black Achievers trip through the South. We made stops in Georgia, Tennessee, and Mississippi. One of our last stops on that trip was to Xavier University of Louisiana (XULA), a HBCU in New Orleans. After we got to our hotel that night, I called my father from a payphone in the lobby to check in. I was expecting the usual "How's it going?", but instead my dad opened with an unexpected question.

"Did you know your mom got her own apartment?"

I didn't. How could I have? The confusion and betrayal in his voice made me nauseous. Stunned and hurt, all I could say was, "Dad, what? What do you mean?"

Dad wasn't about to explain anything over the phone. He ended the call abruptly, saying, "I'll tell you more when you get home."

Looking back now, starting around the time I was ten years old there were occasional signs that my mother was drifting. She would go on unpredictable and what felt like unprovoked fits of rearranging everything in our rooms during the day when we were at school or when we were away visiting relatives. If she greeted us in the afternoon announcing, "I cleaned your rooms!", I would walk upstairs in dread. What she had actually done was pull everything, every article of clothing, every shoe, blanket, and pillow off of every surface, leaving a jumbled pile of things. By the time I was in tenth grade, she was completely gone. She never made it to my sisters' eighth-grade graduation. I remember immediately after their graduation ceremony, my dad asked if I thought it would be all right for my sisters to go to their friends' house to celebrate. Because my mom wasn't there, he was turning to me to make parenting decisions. I didn't become his surrogate spouse, but by age fifteen I became one of his friends, a confidante who was like a thought partner to him. This is what I remember.

By the time I got back from the Black Achievers trip everything had completely fallen apart. When I walked in and set down my bags my dad offered me and my sisters a devastating choice: we could go and live with our mom or we could stay with him. In my math she had abandoned us all and my dad, despite being openly broken in spirit, was still thinking of us. We all chose to stay with him.

Left alone to care for his family, my father struggled in profound ways. He was trying to pay the bills on one salary and that meant pulling a lot of overtime to make it all work out, which required him to work seven days a week. As the shock of my mother's exodus wore off, I think he was met with the despair that only those who have once been abandoned know. He had been there before, when he was a boy and his parents left him to his grandparents' care. Experiencing the grief of being abandoned once more, Dad fell into a downward spiral. He turned to the community that he had known the longest, his cousins. Unfortunately, their world was soaked in substance use and the traps of addiction.

The contrast could not have been more dramatic. Once my parents had converted to Islam, our household did not even permit the consumption of alcohol. In the '70s, my father had experimented with drugs like pot and mushrooms, but with marriage and family, he'd left all of that behind. Now, for solace and companionship, he went back to self-medicating, first with alcohol and eventually with crack cocaine. I was a D.A.R.E kid, passionately opposed to any drug use. What I witnessed with my dad was how fragile we all are and just how debilitating depression can be. I also witnessed how substance use becomes substance abuse nearly immediately. He claimed his first time using crack cocaine was no big deal. But the high he experienced on his second exposure launched him into a seventeen-year quest to reach that same euphoria again. His chase taught me that addiction is not a moral failing, but a physiological and mental illness that can take anyone by surprise. As a consequence, my sense of Grant Boulevard as a place of security and ease, eroded.

Through this time of transition, he managed to hold on to his post office job; he was focused that way. He had a behind-the-scenes job where the workplace culture was one of tolerance and solidarity and grace. The crew would routinely party on the job and Dad could be counted on to be the life of the party—singing, dancing, and keeping the beat going. His genuinely likable personality protected him, as did his coworkers. A number of the workers were military veterans, some damaged from their time in Vietnam or the Korean War, struggling with their own emotional trauma. The dock ran with lax rules that looked the other way when employees were sleeping on the job or otherwise impaired. And his coworkers covered for each other when one or the other was having an especially bad day. This was their workplace culture. My father was living through a mental and physiological health crisis, but instead of intervening, his employer continued to show him grace.

Like so many of my ancestors, when my family core split open, I began to find ways to disappear to protect myself. I coped by learning how to be in a room and not be seen, how to camouflage myself when I was in any environment. It's important to recognize that my family dissolution was happening in my early teen years, when I was a high school student. We look at teenagers and presume them to be young adults, but they are more young than they are adults. I became a kid trying to survive. Elementary school had been paradise. Middle school marked the beginning of my experience of being taunted for being different. But having to be bussed to an all-White suburb for high school that following year was just too much.

I was among the early generation of kids who were bussed an hour each way to suburban public schools. The Milwaukee Public School System paid our tuition with the intention of giving us—that is, urban Black kids—access to a higher-quality education. The program, an early version of charter schools, was called Chapter 220. It existed to give access and to force integration. Whitefish Bay was an affluent community that had so much more than my neighborhood school could offer in terms of programming, teacher training, and facilities. It was a beautiful, pristinely landscaped, safe campus with modern, well-equipped classrooms, and a ridiculous indoor pool. Students were trusted and thereby permitted to leave campus for an hour at lunch time every day. The cumulative effect of such safety, rich resources, and freedom was like being in a foreign country. The language was different, the style was different, the sense of ease and leisure was so different. As a result, the thirty or so Black kids from all across the North Side stood out like foreigners. We were a tribe within a nation, and the nation of predominantly white locals made it clear that we were tourists, allowed to pass through but not to stay. Even the teachers made us feel wholly unwelcome. It was obvious from the start that the North Side kids hadn't had the same academic preparation as the suburban kids. We were extra work, a burden on teachers who didn't want to slow down their semester plan to accommodate us. I was not made to feel like my ideas or experiences mattered. I was not made to feel like I was of any value.

Adding to my discomfort was the fact that although my mother had left us, she was still trying in her own way to stay involved. She didn't want me to have to take the bus, so she insisted on driving me. But she was always late—not by a few minutes, but by thirty to forty-five minutes, and she would often break down in tears during the trip. Every time she drove me to school, I was late. And every time I was late resulted in being kept after for school detention. I didn't know what to do about any of this and so I endured the suburban mirage of Whitefish Bay for two school years.

To try to ease my situation, my dad gave me permission to stop covering myself with a headscarf. That seemed to give me license to change dramatically, so I threw myself into the social mainstream. It was the first time I went to school without wearing a headscarf. I learned to cultivate relationships with people who had a lot more social capital, like the girls who dated the football team. I became a cheerleader and even managed to get asked to the prom as a freshman, which created somewhat of a social scandal.

Still, life was hard for me—the commute, the culture, the constant feeling of coming up short of expectations. At the end of tenth grade, I made a decision on my own. I set out to discover what I needed to do to transfer to a high school on the North Side. I got the papers I needed, forged my parents' signatures, and submitted them myself. The fall of my eleventh-grade year, I landed at Washington High, a school two blocks from where I lived. We passed through metal detectors to access the building, all the windows had bars on them, all the doors had alarms, the cafeteria was sterile and ugly, and there was certainly no Olympic sized swimming pool. Our extra resource was an onsite day care center---the North Side of Milwaukee at that time had the highest teenage pregnancy rate in the country. School officials hoped that by providing day care in the building, more of these teen moms would at least get a high school diploma. Every day was a different kind of struggle than what I'd experienced at Whitefish Bay. My class started with 400 students, but only a portion of us made it to graduation.

By eleventh grade I was binge drinking and smoking a lot of marijuana, floating through a labyrinth of incredibly dangerous situations—house parties where gun shots were fired, predation by much-older men trying to convert me and other girls my age into stripping and sex work. But I was lucky: I had Tamara.

Tamara became my best friend, and she had these big, sheltering wings. No matter the circumstance I was never truly alone because I had her friendship. This friendship became a sisterhood and her family became my family. Tamara's mother, Teresa, also took to protecting and providing for me. And when I say, "took me in," I may as well say she adopted me. I called her Umi, which means mother and was what her other children called her. In the shelter of this family, I never had to ask for food or pay bills. I was an equal in that house. When I needed a place to stay, I slept on their couch and I contributed as a member of the family.

Even with Umi's guardianship, I barely graduated from high school. In my social circle were slightly older college students who were studying in Kansas, and when on a whim they said I could hang out with them there, I took them up on it and caught a bus out of state. I spent nearly a month living in Kansas without sending word to anyone back home. It wasn't until Umi's family sent an email to an AOL account trying to contact me that I figured out how strange that was. Their message to me was clear: "If we don't hear from you, we're going to file a missing person's report." I called Umi and her husband and let them know I was fine and would return to Milwaukee. I had missed so much school by then that only through the intervention of one of my teachers was I barely able to graduate.

It's still really shocking to me how quickly our family disintegrated. Our world completely fell apart and no one really even knew it. We had been that rare Black family that had beat the odds and arrived into the American middle class. We had transcended. I had no way of seeing just how rare we were in the '80s, or just how fragile our world actually was. At the time I did not fully understand that both my parents had already experienced and survived abandonment themselves. They were still living with the fallout from their own shattered families. We were all trapped in a cycle, a new generation of family collapse. Despite this, all was not lost. My sisters both went on to earn impressive degrees. My father escaped the traps of addiction and became a savant in the stock market. My mother chose to go back to school where she earned her BA, an MA, and is now starting to think about Ph.D. programs. Both my maternal grandmothers lived into older age with a rare autonomy. They continued to reimagine themselves as adults, pursuing their own financial and personal independence. Both retired late in life—my paternal grandmother at seventy-five from nursing, and my maternal grandmother at eighty years old. And while each of them were met with incredible challenges in moving forward with their freedom, they never stopped making the choice to pursue it. They, in that way, are like so many of us all.

What I have come to realize is that everyone in our lives is making choices based on what they think is still yet possible, based on what they in their souls are yearning for. We're all navigating what we think the options are and what we think the outcomes may be. We're all calculating our odds. We're all trying to be strategic about what is the next best thing for us. We often mimic the choices we've seen others make, including those who have been toxic to themselves and their loved ones. We're all trying to just get ahead.

When she moved out, my mother didn't know she was risking separating herself from her children forever in some ways. My dad couldn't conceive of the consequences of his addiction, or what it would be like for his daughters to witness him struggle. We're shortsighted that way. It's a universal human failing. It's so hard for us to persistently see beyond ourselves.

My teachers at Washington High School laid out the next path for me by convincing me I had a choice. I did not have to give up; I did not have to be crushed by the weights of abandonment. College was my way out. Going to college meant leaving my family and its complications behind, and ultimately that's what I chose. I wanted and needed to be far away. I moved to Louisiana, where I didn't know a single person and where no one knew me. My coping mechanism was escape. Fleeing Milwaukee was also my path to radically reimagining what was possible.

## Key Takeaways:

- **When people let you down, and they will, you're actually being given an opportunity to find your own way, and your own joy. There is power in this.**
- **Don't be afraid to do what you need to do to survive and thrive, even if it means breaking with the established norms.**
- **Stepping into the unknown helps you find the path of self-discovery. This is the zone where powerful learning happens.**

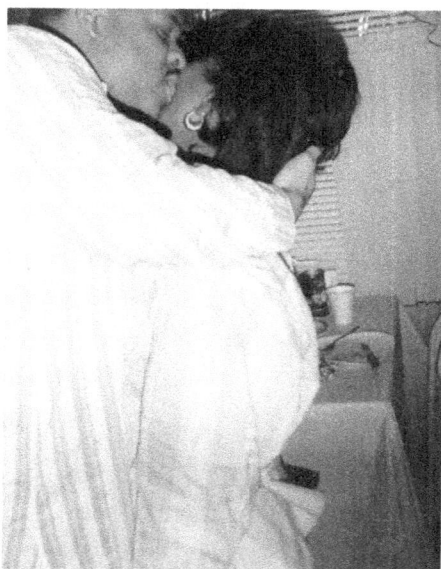

# CHAPTER THREE
## Strong Women Rescued Me

When I was a little girl, spending hours sitting alone, surrounded by books on the floor of the Washington Park Library children's reading room, was one of my favorite places to be. I was a huge fan of a series popular then called *Choose Your Own Adventure*. In summary, each story was written from a second-person point of view, with the reader positioned as the main character and empowered to make choices which determined the direction of the pilot. It was endlessly entertaining to surrender my imagination to stories full of suspenseful moments and then, as a reader, get to decide what I thought should happen next. There were no wrong answers and no tragic endings, just exciting options. Each vignette listed multiple choices. Depending on what you picked (if, for example, you chose to "cross the river by bridge"), you were told what the outcome would be ( "jump to page 87") and your journey of discovery would either continue or come to an abrupt (and sometimes tragic) end.

I read these books over and over again, truly delighted by getting to pick new routes leading to new outcomes all contained within the same book jacket. It's safe to say I liked the feeling of independence that these books provided, and of being in some small way in control of my own direction.

This series taught me a lot about the core principles of travel, experimentation, and design. As a child, I believed that the real world operated by the same pragmatic logic: yes, at times the wrong decision was made. But you could always begin again. Sure, despite your best efforts, you could get hopelessly lost or miss an opportunity, but you could always recover.

As it were, I was miraculously fortunate to have several grownups in my life who, simply put, guided me when I needed guidance, and saved me when I lost my way and needed new direction. I've already mentioned Umi, but her story deserves more detail. My mother worked with Umi at a nonprofit center for women victimized by domestic violence in the early '90s. Umi's daughter and I became friends and, over time, sisters. I was accepted and then folded into the mix of her family. At the same time, my mother was wilting in her life and also in mine. Umi, however, was only getting stronger. She embodied so much of '70s Black culture, as a groovy Black woman with an Afro hairstyle (when the vibe felt right), and who, among other roles, owned and operated a Black art framing business in the basement of her home. As my mother was withdrawing, Umi offered a constant stream of light in the form of positive Black identity. She was growing in her sense of self-possession, political activism, and preserved sensuality. Umi was so open to making a seat for me in her lively, loving household that at age seventeen, I left my parents' home and went to live with Umi and her family of five for several months. It says something about her that although she was not Muslim— her birth name was Teresa—her kids chose to call her Umi, an Arabic word for mother. She added an invaluable second set of flavors to who I am today. I didn't get to choose that my mom was going to choose an adventure that took her away from me, and I didn't choose the arrival of Umi. Fortunately, Umi chose me as another daughter.

Had I stayed at Whitefish Bay High School, it's hard to imagine just how different the story of my life might be. But because I chose my own adventure, forging my parents' signatures on the transfer forms that enabled me to jump to Washington High School for my junior year, my prospects got a lot brighter in surprising ways. Umi's other daughter was in school there, and I knew she would be a social anchor for me. So, I transferred myself to a new school.

At Washington High School, set against the depressing trends of declining graduation rates and increasing teen pregnancies in Milwaukee, some key teachers and a guidance counselor embraced me. A Black woman, an Indian woman, and a White woman were the diverse coalition of females who helped me survive. They were all self-assured and each deeply compassionate women in their forties and fifties. They were confidantes and coaches, advisers, teachers, and cheerleaders. Collectively, they were able to cast a wide net to catch me and to keep me from falling through the cracks. They invested their time in me, making it clear that I was going to make it despite all the chaos, and in letting me know how much they believed in me. They were the manifestation of the notion that I could in fact empower myself in some ways, that I could choose my own adventure. Especially in the vulnerable and confusing teenage years, it's so hard to move beyond personal setbacks and to figure out how to protect your own optimism. These empathetic and resilient women got me to believe that even though my family life was in shambles, it did not mean all was lost for me.

In fact, they helped me to understand that "this hard place you're in is where you are. It doesn't have to be where you end up." It was the spirit of these women who saw in me a part of themselves that tethered them to my journey and that connected us. They, too, like all of us at some point, had experienced loneliness, abandonment, and hopelessness.

Looking back, there could have been a moat of disengagement and self-protection that might have caused me to reject them. But they kept showing up and I needed them. Their seeing eyes carried me across tumultuous waters.

My eleventh-grade English teacher, Mrs. Smith, created a safe place for me to talk about all the difficult things I was living, and all the beautiful things about big ideas and poetry. In my senior year, my AP English teacher, Miss Anton, was from India. Her classroom was where controversy lived alongside nuance and empathy. She was probably why I became an English major in college. She revealed to me the tremendous power innate in stories and how classrooms could be sacred places for courageous conversations. I wasn't there often—I skipped a *lot* of school, but when I was there, there was always a rigorous conversation happening.

Once, when I ran off to Kansas City to chase after a college girl I was dating, I missed nearly a month of classes. School policy stated that any student missing that many weeks could not pass the class. Ms. Anton never judged me for missing school, and she covered for me. She always welcomed me when I reappeared. To each of her graduating seniors, Ms. Anton sent a final farewell letter. What I remember of her letter captured her kindness. She said about me, "When you came, it counted." She valued having me whenever I could figure out how to be present.

Mrs. Brunson had the burdensome job of being a guidance counselor at Washington High School. She had a raspy smoker's voice that always reminded me of the "Big Marge" character in the movie *Peewee Herman's Big Adventure*, and big, curly hair. Mrs. Brunson was an irresistible force of tough love and helpful energy. She was always very frank with me about my future. She had "seeing eyes" that convinced me of what she was already certain of. She pulled me into her small office on more than one occasion to read me the riot act when I missed school or got a failing grade. She told me I wasn't going to get stuck in the odds of the North Side. She told me that I was going to make it—someone who said, "You're going to college, Kimberly." Mrs. Brunson could see my potential and had no qualms about shoving me toward it.

In that way, she helped me with my college applications and got me registered for the ACT exam. I had no one else to help me navigate my way out and away. She stepped in to support me, powered by her full faith in a potential I couldn't see. Because of her encouragement and commitment, I could accept there were possibilities that included my Black and queer identities. Too many Black kids never even get a glimpse of a larger world. Mrs. Brunson was the one who helped me see that I was worthy of undiscovered paths. She made it possible to envision another route to travel than the dead ends I saw all around me.

College was the path these caring women were trying to get me on. They were all college educated, so to them this was what you did to build a future. I didn't choose those women. They were sent into my life. Things that are given can be accepted or rejected, so that's a form of choice, too. Their unwavering belief that somehow I was going to beat the odds was just the push I needed. They knew I was going to make it out and they convinced me I could.

While each of these women had my back, they also required me to do what I could to help myself. They pushed me to be much more resourceful and helped me to learn the language of self-advocacy. They were all willing to point me in the right direction, but I was going to have to keep reaching up, finding whatever additional resources I needed. They never made me feel guilty or incapable. They never asked me how leaving Milwaukee for college was going to impact anyone else but me. They never made me feel ashamed for wanting something more.

By the time I was ready to apply to colleges, I had already been to a number of college campuses with the Black Achievers' program. I knew quite a bit about the application process—I was going to have to go through a director of admissions, submit various forms, and write an essay. Fortunately, I already had enough exposure to wrap my mind around how to gain entrance to the distant world of college.

I started looking at schools in the South. Louisiana State University (LSU) in New Orleans held a special appeal. Louisiana was, for me, a full-fledged foreign country, its exotic nature evident in its architecture, music, dance, food, and customs. New Orleans was where Europe met the first peoples of the Americas, and where they met folks from the African diaspora. I knew I couldn't afford to study abroad, so I applied to LSU as the next most foreign experience I could just maybe access.

When LSU's offer to join the freshman class came through, my dad packed up his Jeep Cherokee and, with his girlfriend along, drove me to Baton Rouge. I had one suitcase. Dad took me to the store to buy dorm supplies of cleaning products and sheets. He dropped me off at my dorm with $50 and good-luck wishes. That $50 went into a bank account to which I added the few hundred I'd saved from summer jobs. Then, I set up a PO box in the student union in case anyone wanted to contact me. With these practical matters settled, I took on more personal challenges.

I walked down the dorm hallway to find my room. I had no one to call to say, "Hey, I've arrived." I remember cleaning all the surfaces, then realizing that I hadn't been assigned a roommate and that I was alone. I cried and cried and cried. I felt terrified and overwhelmed with loneliness. But I didn't surrender. Instead, I wrote my name on every whiteboard on every dorm door on my floor. "Hi! I'm Kimberly from Wisconsin. Come say hi." I survived by building relationships, ingratiating myself to people who knew more than I knew and had more than I had.

That first year, I did a lot of following folks around—kids from Texas, Mississippi, Arkansas, and of course, Louisiana. I was like a tag-along kid and I learned a lot about White Southerner culture during that first year. One of my most significant teachers arrived during my second semester in the form of Kari Ann, a White girl from Picayune, Mississippi. The very first time I talked to her, she was generous with her counsel. "You have to watch out for the niggers here. You have to be really careful around niggers. His pants are gonna be low and he's gonna talk so sweet, but you have to avoid him." Her words were coated in sugar. She truly intended to offer me a loving warning. I later found out I was only the second Black girl she had ever really known. She thought of me primarily as a (Black) Northerner who needed protection from Black boys, whom she had been taught to believe were dangerous. I knew I needed to make this relationship work, and it required me to become an instant anthropologist. I was studying this Southern culture from a place of observation. I learned a lot about the power of cultural conditioning and racial bias from her, but I also learned about loyal love.

On school breaks, Kari Ann always invited me to her family home. Her family saw me as an exceptional Black person, as in *the* exception. They held deeply racist views, but for reasons I'll never fully understand, they fully accepted me. Their story got more unpredictable when I met her parents, two men living in the Deep South in the 1990s. They were both nurses, able to afford a house with a pool. When I was around them, I was a member of the family, an equal child who called them both "Dad." When I wasn't around, people who looked like me were all the "n-word." In the contradictory spirit that is human nature, these gay men provided for me. They gave me money to go home, bought me groceries, fussed and worried over me. The irony and limits of their liberalism were never lost on me, and it never made me love the two of them any less. It's a challenging dynamic to understand, but I think that's true of most family dynamics.

Back at college, I chose English as my major since it had been my favorite subject in high school. To me, literature represented all that I learned about people—all their stories—and I loved books. At LSU, I was going to explore all the stories the American South could offer me in terms of strangeness. Always in search of resources and connection, I continued to build out my network. I joined the first Black sorority, Alpha Kappa Alpha, full of strong Black women from all over the South. I traveled to events across the region that gave me a different sense of America. But even more valuable to me, AKA gave me a second community of sisters.

Meanwhile, I began to think about a career. I first thought of going to medical school—I liked helping people and the prestige of the title, but like many before me, bombing out of my first chemistry class killed that possibility. Uncertain what to do, but knowing I had to do something soon, a poster in LSU's Hatcher Hall caught my eye. It advertised a master's degree fellowship program in education. It was a one-year program, and I liked teaching, so this seemed like a low-level commitment that would buy me some time and earn me a degree I could use anywhere. Plus, if I got into the fellowship program, it would be a free degree. Bonus. Well, I got the fellowship and fell headlong into a whirlwind of teaching and learning. Days, I taught in a public grade school. Evenings, I immersed myself in the totally absorbing study of educational theory. I was hooked.

Through this almost accidental fellowship I fell in absolute love with teaching, and I purposely chose to get a degree that would have international application. My good fortune landing in this program was finding a curriculum and a faculty that encouraged interdisciplinary study, exploring the intersections and the energy around collaboration. It felt like joining a family of the best, most creative, accepting, and positive kind.

The program was incredibly rigorous and demanding—the days were long and required each of us to teach during the day and then to be in grad classes four nights a week, but I was used to working hard. I got my first job at thirteen and had a pretty long history of employment. I had been, at one time or another, a child-care attendant at a nonprofit, a sales clerk at the Body Shop, and counter help at Blockbuster Video. Other less-successful gigs included being a waitress for one day and a grocery store checkout girl for two days—a career in food was not in my future, but teaching most obviously was.

I wanted to spend more time with other educators and theorists after completing the master's program, but I needed a paying job. At twenty-one, I started teaching full-time at a public middle school in East Baton Rouge Parish and continued going to school at night. I figured out that if I rolled right into the Ph.D program at LSU, I could get a Ph.D by the time I turned twenty-seven. I went on to study curriculum theory, which intrigued me. The study of theory became a longer adventure of thinking about identity development, equity, and how teachers could be facilitators for discovery all from the front of the room. I wanted to explore how to cultivate teachers who could show up for kids who needed them the most. I wanted to pioneer approaches that might be able to reach kids like me.

It took seven years from the first year of undergrad for me to complete my PhD. It was a marathon run at a sprinter's clip. I was always figuring out how to make a living for myself, how to make every action count, how to make every paper publishable, and how to stack one achievement as a step to the next. I was still operating in survival mode. I had a sharp mindfulness for efficiency because I felt I didn't have money or time to waste. Besides, I was beginning to prepare myself to take even bigger leaps and to become an even more self-defined, self-sufficient woman.

## Key Takeaways:

- **Immerse yourself in supportive communities—they give you the water and light you need to thrive.**
- **Women are nurturers. Treat yourself to the company of incredible women and honor their time.**
- **Accept help, but commit to acting with discipline so that you are prepared to also help yourself.**
- **Once you find what speaks to you, go all in.**

# CHAPTER FOUR
## Wanting More From Work

Despite a full-on sprint through graduate school and a PhD program in curriculum and design, I never specifically set it as an intention to become a secondary education teacher. Before I started teaching middle-school English at twenty-one and while I was still a grad student, I had some generalized ambitions to become a lawyer, a judge, or perhaps in a world where passing chemistry didn't matter, a doctor. It's fair to say that I wanted my career to be a force for the common good. Seeing a posting for a fellowship that would enable me to stay in Louisiana and earn a "free" advanced degree ushered me into a world of teaching that felt like the perfect coincidence.

I kept saying "yes" to signs like the fellowship, and these signs have been a larger guidepost in my life's journey. Listening to these subtle invitations from a force that has always felt nurturing and reliable led me into a most sacred space: the classroom. In a classroom, you're trying to create trust and safety and vulnerability and openness in the heart space. Every day you are invited to work with people with the primary goal of enabling them to be more thoughtful about, well, everything—that's a sacred exchange. You ask them to be present with you and with each other, to give the best that they can in the brief time that you share together, and to be their best selves despite whatever else might be swirling in their minds and worlds. There is a magic to being an excellent teacher. For all of us fortunate to have had one, this is something we know to be undeniably true.

Many of my own teachers had these superpowers, and their impact on me was impossible to measure. They had given me, a child and teenager facing a lot of unusual challenges, a base on which to stand and a vision for survival. I always felt honored to be seen as someone's teacher. When a child or a young adult looks you in the eye and says to you outright, "You taught me something," it affirms that they were made to feel safe. It also confirms that they were able to move from a place of discomfort (the unknown) to comfort, from a perspective that felt certain into a new perspective entirely. That they trusted you enough to allow you to take them on a journey and that they allowed you to walk with them. This, for a true teacher, is a moment of tremendous gratification. In those moments I felt certain that by choosing to be an educator that I was surrendering to a calling if you will, to serve as a steward..

I was twenty-three years old when I entered the PhD program and aside from my professors, I had never personally known anyone with a doctoral degree. This was another chance to "choose my own adventure." I concentrated on exploring educational theory and what the study of it could mean for academically talented kids who were outliers like me, different because of race, gender, family of origin, religion, or other diverse identities. Meanwhile, I became certified to teach English and I joined the faculty of a public magnet school in Baton Rouge. The student population there was equally divided between neighborhood kids and talented kids bussed from all across the city. My students were all identified as gifted, which also meant that ninety-nine percent of them came from outside of the neighborhood. All of them, in fact, except a young man named Kevin, but that's a different beautiful story.

After my disastrous experience as a bussed kid at Whitefish Bay, I felt deeply in touch with the challenges of this divided population. The neighborhood students were almost entirely Black and working-class, while the students in the magnet program were from all over the world. Many of their parents were professors at LSU or graduates of the university. Most of them were middle- and upper-class. It was a complicated arrangement.

My grandmother still lived in South Philly, and I had some experience with the city, so moving there to teach in an urban school seemed like a good idea. I posted my résumé on a job board for teachers and got a call right away from a suburban school superintendent. During my interview, the superintendent laid out the situation plainly.

"Kimberly, we don't have many students of color. We have no faculty of color. That's the environment you're walking into. If you take this job this is what I can pay you."

I appreciated his candor and the fact that the salary was double what I was making in Baton Rouge. It wasn't at all the urban school I'd assumed I'd work for, but I jumped in anyway. It turned out to be a good fit. I taught there for the next eighteen years.

My many years of classroom experience taught me that teaching is about being a social worker, cheerleader, creative director, thought leader, and temperature-setter and checker. Being a teacher is the art of tracking all the instruments in the room, knowing the music, and conducting a symphony. It's being able to really see and listen to people, being able to encourage people. Little did I realize how teaching was shaping my business leadership style. Deliberately looking back on how I was able to navigate my way through changing environments, changing times, and changing student populations, I see how it all contributed to my confidence as a leader. I saw that I could manage my way through a lot of hard, unpredictable stuff in a way that was authentically my own. Along the way, I was able to co-design and co-teach interdisciplinary courses in colonialism and in marginalization in the American story. Those years taught me about planning with the end in mind, an approach called "backward design," and to move with a mindfulness for desired outcomes. These are skills that will be with me always, as will the memories of the relationships I nurtured. It was inspiring and incredibly powerful work.

But after twelve years in the classroom, the time began to feel right for a teaching sabbatical—a privileged chance to detach from the daily routine to see beyond it. It meant being able to safely leave my role as teacher for a semester to study creativity and to travel. Visiting Africa called to me.

I had no contacts, no familiarity, no experience to support me on my planned solo travels in Kenya. When I landed in Nairobi, I had no local currency and no formal visa—only a receipt showing I had applied and paid for one. A woman from Luxembourg who'd befriended me on the flight from Istanbul offered to give me a ride to my hotel. From there, I spent the next week walking twelve miles or more a day around the city, including Kibera, a vast community that is one of the largest urban slums in all of Africa. Over the next two weeks spent traveling around the country, I saw what living on a dollar a day and a sparse diet looked like. I came across a nonprofit established to help victims of female genital mutilation and HIV whose communities had ostracized them, and young elephants orphaned by human habitat encroachment and poachers. It was an intense time of seeing a whole different level of "otherness" and need.

Once I got back home, filmmaker Ava Duvernay's documentary *13th,* about the perversion of the Thirteenth Amendment, had just been released. What arose from the Emancipation Proclamation, an agreement designed by President Lincoln, also offered a loophole allowing someone who broke the law to be captured and used for slave labor. It was used to arrest people for being unemployed if they were resting on the streets longer than an allotted time. The right to learn to read was withheld, making it impossible to fully participate in society and in the economy. Duvernay argues convincingly that it was a setup for the entire criminal justice system that we have today and the persistent trauma of incarceration. I cried through most of it, but was especially crushed by what Khalif Browder, a young man wrongly arrested for petty theft in 2010 when he was sixteen years old and held for three years at Rikers Island in New York, had to suffer through. I was so hurt knowing he, still a child, had been forced to spend two of those years in solitary confinement, all because his family couldn't post his bail. Coupled with my travels in Nairobi, I had become a witness to so much deep complexity and profound dysfunction.

In 2017, the massive problems in our society were quickly mounting. Black folks couldn't gain access to equitable education or find living wage work, and they still can't. The traps of poverty, the long- and short-term consequences of social injustice, and the data around the climate catastrophe were all coming into fuller view for me. Some thinking was emerging about the need for solutions that were bigger, cross-disciplinary, and "intersectional." The problems and the possibilities for solutions seemed like new signposts for my journey of trying to figure out what I was being called to do, of where I was being directed to show up. How could

I move from what I observed in the world to help me show up in a meaningful, positive, impactful way?

A daring idea began to take shape in my mind, a notion that I could create equitable jobs through sustainable fashion. Even though I'd been raised by strong, stylish women and a mother who expertly made special-occasion clothes, I had no direct experience in the fashion industry.

I still don't fully understand why I had the temerity (a powerful word in Harper Lee's *To Kill a Mockingbird*—a novel I had shared with hundreds of students) to think I should start a business that had the potential, by design, to tackle huge problems. Being Black and Muslim, wearing a scarf as a child, dealing with family fractures and personal loss taught me a lot about moving through space with a strong sense of temerity. Although I frequently felt it in crushing waves, I never let fear paralyze me. Instead, I launched Grant Blvd with a never-tried-before vision for changing the conversation and creating an enduring impact.

I began the leap to building a business five years before I moved into the "house" of entrepreneurship. To continue the metaphor, when I got ready to move into my new life, that structure of entrepreneurship barely had walls. I was abandoning the lushly gilded cage of my comfortable, lucrative, secure teaching gig—working nine months of the year, making six figures with great health care, a pension plan, and a great deal of classroom autonomy. This teaching job, coupled with my dedication to living far below my means, had given me total freedom from financial worries. As an adult, unlike during my financially precarious teen and young adult years, I never ever thought about money. I lived frugally with the intention that I could be free of money anxiety out in the world. The hardest thing about leaving my career was figuring out how I would cope with stepping into abject financial uncertainty for myself and my daughter. I would have to move in the way pioneers do.

I didn't know what would happen if I left. But I knew if I stayed, my wings were never going to grow any more in that comfortable cage. Its familiar walls would keep me at a certain size, smaller than I somehow had faith to believe I could be. Although the future was, as it always is, totally unknown, I knew that I had to step up and out if I were ever to meet my own full potential. I was going to have to fully invest in and bet on myself.

As a child I was always taking care of myself, and I have come to realize that the practice of self-care became a form of investing in myself. Self-care for me means more than physical wellness. I gave myself permission to invest the money I earned in what I wanted. For me, that was rarely material objects. Taking classes and traveling to twenty-four countries were the major investments that helped change my view of what I could and should be.

I returned to what I knew by way of how to learn: I went back to school. I took a class on the business of fashion to frame a way of thinking about my response to economic and environmental problems. What I learned exposed the horror of the fashion industry in just about every way—unfair labor practices, unsustainable resource use, devastating waste generation, and thoughtless consumerism. To learn more about incarceration, I started volunteering at Books Through Bars, a West Philadelphia nonprofit that for more than thirty years has been sending free books to incarcerated people in six mid-Atlantic states (Pennsylvania, New York, New Jersey, Delaware, Maryland, and Virginia). Books Through Bars' mission is to support self-determination, self-education, and healing behind bars by fulfilling inmate requests for books. My experience with this program became a foundation for a decision to build something with a focus on service to the formerly incarcerated. It also helped me to build a community of practice anchored in service and led me toward a life-changing moment of leadership inside of a men's correctional facility.

During this phase of exploration I spent time getting to know people personally familiar with these kinds of environments. Learning to listen in deference. By deepening my understanding of who I might be able to help, I hoped to build a business on a rock of knowledge and faith, not on a shifting foundation of sands made from superficial feelings of goodwill. It meant committing to just keep going, keep listening, being aware, open, and curious. It's a journey of seeing the world as it is and recognizing what matters to you, then figuring out what you can do. I chose to accept the commission to do this work, and it truly felt like an artist's commission. Designing a business of any sort is a blank canvas for your creation.

Conventional business design has always, always been about intention. In our standardized capitalist, Western approach, the due north has always exclusively been creating and then maximizing profit. Everything else gets compromised in service of the bottom line. Concerns about collateral costs to the environment or workers or even consumers are of no or minimal importance. There's a closely guarded mystery around how dark and damaging the practice of leading with profit is for all of us.

I didn't come into entrepreneurship from the classic MBA perspective or the legacy of parents who had made millions in business by exploiting people. What I saw growing up were people in my community who were very small business owners who knew and cared about the neighborhood, and who knew and cared about their customers. In contrast, we're living in a time when people are disconnected from themselves and from each other. I wanted to start a business that would change the economy, not make superficial improvements to social problems. What motivated me was trying to shift consumer thoughts about the goods they consume—about their means of production, their cost to the planet, and their potential to create positive outcomes for people.

How could I build a business on a product that was not based on denying the climate catastrophe or the abuse of women? We're all inundated with messaging that we are not enough and that we don't own enough. So much of our education is focused on stories of negativity and loss. We need to find a balance and learn to recognize that we can have and probably already do have enough. I am trying to encourage people to be intentional about what they consume. To see that out of all the overwhelming choices on offer, you get to choose. As a consumer, you can't necessarily determine what gets produced, but you have power and agency to choose what you will consume and to choose what you will be loyal to.

As I prepared myself to launch a business, I dedicated myself to self-study and to using my teaching practice as an opportunity to present new ways of seeing systems. Through my high school curriculum, I had been teaching about the global supply chain rooted in colonialism. In my eleventh-grade course, we investigated the American quagmire: could a nation whose very growth depended on exploitation and violence claw its way out of relentless destruction, greed, and White supremacist structures? In the classroom, it became clear that the things I cared about most were the human rights of people whose circumstances I could truly see, and the planet I had loved since childhood. It wasn't a personal need that led me to build a business, something I recognize as being a very real and valid reason for many entrepreneurs. Instead, it was my own journey of discovery and an unshakeable sense of concern.

I'd been raised to believe that to know is to do. If you see suffering, injustice, mismanagement, are you just going to be like an ostrich—stick your head in the sand and do nothing? That kind of avoidant thinking has never been part of who I am, and I never wanted it to be the legacy of my story. Walking to a different kind of finish line with a different kind of fight in mind has always called me out of bed. Defining and developing a business that's bold and, in some spaces, radical is a different kind of love story—one of radical love for people and the planet. When you build with purpose it becomes a grueling but inspired journey. And then one day, it becomes an inspiration to others.

For me, the process of designing a company started with a clear statement of values. Transparency, consistency, truthfulness, and creating a culture of care came first. I wanted to invite people to become a part of the build-out of better things. As a company, I knew we needed to aspire to sell beautiful garments, yes, but also more than products. Building a brand dedicated to fostering participation, and to advancing the work of people with a shared sense of commitment in doing better, was and still is an ambitious business plan. My dream was to welcome customers to join my journey to use sustainable design in ways that would make them feel part of a movement. Our garments would be like stylish souvenirs of an entrepreneurial experiment we did together.

Ultimately, what I wanted was for my business to offer the opportunity to belong to a community of employees and customers who were coming together because of their most cherished values. We all want to belong. As a human being you need to be with people. Purpose can be a driver of that unity. What purpose looks like is different for everyone, so finding the right team is essential, but once you find them you feel like you're part of a good fight, anchored to who you want to be. Purpose is part of the anchor of building this team and the element that fuels and helps maintain momentum. And for our community, those values are centered in being seen and celebrated for all the things we are and to be a part of positive solution development, or the light.

Along the way, I've learned that when you design with meaningful purpose as your ultimate due north, you lay the groundwork for something much bigger: a purpose-driven life. Finding your purpose is distinctly personal, but for each of us, this lifestyle choice has the potential to bring us a sense of peace. By understanding Maslow's hierarchy of needs, we see that as people's basic requirements for a safe and secure life are met, they can ascend toward more satisfaction and gratification. In a business structure, that can be achieved by encouraging and enabling employees to grow and self-actualize within the organization. If a company can't give this space, it is much, much harder to hold on to talented, hard-working people. You've got to be able to pay people well enough to retain top talent, but it is also essential to be always tapping into who they are and who they want to be.

For emerging manufacturers like Grant Blvd, part of the challenge is creating a product line that contributes to a basic need in a way that offers customers some experience or some*thing* that helps them feel they are moving closer to being their best self. That can take many forms, from a makeup product, to a wellness service, to a pair of fancy-ass shoes.

Of all the things we can buy, peace is the one that is most difficult to put a value on. But true peace gives you the highest quality of life. When we aspire to something beyond the limited boundary that profit sets, more joy and peace and dignity results. My intention for Grant Blvd was to design a business with future anchored vision, one that defends the needs of all people, and that puts stewardship of the planet at the center of our shared human purpose. That's what makes it so much damn fun.

So, here's something that you don't know. I never thought I was qualified to contribute to any fashion brand. The truth is that I didn't want to be in fashion per se. I didn't grow up obsessed with couture fashion or even with the idea of business ownership. Those weren't things I fantasized about. As a kid I wanted to reduce violence, I wanted to end drug use, and I wanted to protect koalas (those were the days of natural history museum dioramas). But as an adult I wanted to teach, I wanted to help alleviate poverty and to change the course of the conversation around how we were paying wages and taking care of people.

Regardless of my Ph.D and the creation of a beautiful career as a scholar and teacher, imposter syndrome in business was still real for me. I believed I didn't have what it takes to join an established company. For Black women, one of the greatest barriers for entry into anything—higher education, professional employment, executive leadership—is what you're conditioned to believe about your prospects, your potential, and your supports. For me, going my own way felt safer, even though the risks of entrepreneurship, especially for minorities who are much more likely to be under-resourced, are huge. I felt like I might have more control, so I placed my bet on me. The concept of Grant Blvd came about because I was seeing things that were not the same as what most other people saw. I didn't want to convince some established company to operate differently. I felt I was seeing a problem that other people didn't care enough about yet.

I considered starting a nonprofit, but ultimately decided not to because I didn't want to be beholden to having to persistently seek other people's generosity. As a Black woman, I didn't want to manage the emotional burden of having to ask predominantly White audiences for charity. That said,

I have come to appreciate how philanthropy in partnership with social entrepreneurship can be fuel for social-impact businesses. Grant Blvd has benefited significantly from the support of foundations and private lending circles along with community finance organizations and even large corporations who are trying to fulfill their corporate social responsibility (CSR) obligations. Without support from this broad coalition, Grant Blvd would not have happened.

Starting a business that can beat the odds is like climbing a mountain- you need a solid crew, the appropriate gear, and a sense of direction. However, if you can see the topmost peak when you first start out, you might not do it- you might not believe you can ever reach such great heights. But what I've learned is the power of getting to the first plateau, of pausing to look behind you and admire how far you've come and what you've achieved. What are the successes you can claim? What did we as a business do that we said we were going to do? Are we paying a living wage? Are we radically inclusive in hiring? Keeping track of where there has been achievement and celebrating it is essential if you are going to endure.

Going out on your own is hard, lonely, discouraging and quite frankly, consistently overwhelming. There are nights on your adventure when your warming fire goes out, when you're wandering in the wilderness. This is the truth of experimentation. Experimentation is discovery, and it's only when you embrace the spirit of the adventurer, daring to cross the border into an unexpected place, that your journey feels inspired. Pursuing purpose over time generates a wealth of energy that gets offered up to you over and over again. When the work you're doing feels bigger than the product, wells of endurance keep springing up.

But beyond that, belief, faith, and optimism have to be baked into your work. For me, these come from a deep connection to the spiritual—I believe that the forces of good and light are real in nature. I believe good and light are more powerful than the forces of darkness. When I surrender to work with the good, my life will be filled with good and light. That belief assures me that I will always ultimately have enough. The "enough" will come in the form of support, connections, and opportunities that I couldn't have curated on my own. We're always choosing the people, the ideas, and the causes we align with. I work very hard to stay dedicated to a spiritual practice, pursuing forces of good and light.

When a forcefield of negativity comes and criticism rides in on it and I don't know how it's all going to work out, I can sit with those feelings, but I don't absorb them. There's a lot of things I don't know. I'm still growing as a thought leader in business and as an influencer of culture. Every day I'm taking the risk to be public about how I'm experimenting and what I'm learning. What people can see is me watering the seeds of Grant Blvd's potential. My vision is getting ever more clear, but communicating nuanced notions in digestible language continues to present challenges.

My approach has rested on trusting that I'm going to be okay, that it's going to all come together just when and how it needs to, especially if I manage to hold the balance of keeping my chin down and simultaneously keeping my head up. I've become a person rooted in a spirit of pragmatic optimism. That faith and optimism is undoubtedly anchored in the longer legacy of all the people who have come before me, the generations of Black folk who had to persist despite their race, gender, abilities, and all other forms of barriers. They were able to rise because they committed to persistence and optimism and to making it another day. Sometimes that meant doing the basics—keeping the lights on another day, feeding their kids another day. They were always standing in full recognition that they wouldn't struggle always. I'm certain you have people like that in your story as well.

In the next chapter, I'm going to share some of what I've learned in my business leadership journey as I began to see all the beautiful possibilities yet discovered.

## Key Takeaways:

- **Say "Yes" to opportunity.**
- **Whatever your role, express your whole self in your work.**
- **Expand your awareness of the world to include big problems and inspire big dreams.**
- **To know is to do—a purpose-driven life of optimism and faith will sustain you.**

# CHAPTER FIVE
## Becoming an Entrepreneur: Lessons Learned

At the heart of B Corp™ and its nonprofit certification arm, B Lab, is a single mantra- "Make Business a Force for Good." In 2006 co-founders Jay Coen Gilbert, Bart Houlahan, and Andrew Kassoy began contemplating how the way businesses think and act needed to be radically transformed if businesses were to be held to higher standards for social and environmental impact, and if they were required to provide accountability and transparency in their operations. Coen is a co-founder of a successful basketball apparel company, AND1, and Houlahan was its CFO/COO. After selling AND1, they joined forces with Kassoy, a Wall Street investment banker who shared their values and vision, to launch B Lab. Its goal was lofty from the start—nothing short of "transforming the global economy to benefit all people, communities, and the planet."[2]

It's a happy coincidence for me that B Lab and B Corp got their start just outside of Philadelphia. By 2023 the B Corp network listed more than 6,700 businesses operating

---

2    B Lab Global website

in 90 countries across 161 industries[3]. Even more businesses of all sizes and types, roughly 150,000 of them, rely on the B Impact Assessment digital tool as a benchmark for setting, measuring, and improving on impact standards that bring about positive economic systems change.

That sounds like a big deal, and it is. You may think, "Who are these companies?" Well, here are two early adopters you're sure to recognize: Patagonia and Ben & Jerry's. In each case the founders, Yvon Chouinard at Patagonia and Ben Cohen and Jerry Greenfield at Ben & Jerry's, were "reluctant" entrepreneurs. They wanted to make superior products, respectively climbing apparel and ice cream, but they were uncomfortable with the standard capitalist approach of aiming to make as much money as possible, whatever it took. For Chouinard it was his deep love of nature that led him to create an environmentally conscious business. For Cohen and Greenfield, creating delicious ice cream with a people-centered business model was a way to serve their communities through social activism (and humor!).

I've talked to too many business leaders who began new ventures without reflecting on some really key questions. Instead, in their haste they begin with questions of logistics. This is a pragmatic approach, but a problematic place to start. To be clear, often the first inquiry that new entrepreneurs ask is "How exactly do I start a business?" There are, of course, many, many possible directions that responses to that question could take. But there are three key questions most people forget to ask next, and which, in my experience, are actually far more important to ask *and* answer before you make any other moves:

1. Who are you presently? Can you be honest with yourself and others about who you've been?

---

[3]    B Corp website

2. How does this business meet a clear psychological need for my target consumer?

3. How can this business, and I as an extension of it, create a positive impact on my community of origin and/or my community of residence?

Answering these questions gives you an important context into what you have to offer in fuller terms. How you respond to these inquiries has the power to set up the drivers for your business design from the onset, as well as to clarify how your business might intentionally align with your wider search for purpose. Your answers make a lot of difference in figuring out your next steps, especially for women and most especially for women of color. These are the questions central to building a business that creates impact and can endure.

Next, there are the classic entrepreneur's questions that absolutely everyone should be able to answer clearly and honestly before getting started in a business.

1. Who is my target consumer?

2. Why is this offering of value to them now?

3. Why am I the right/best person to make this offering?

The earlier chapters of this book revealed to you quite a bit about who I am because I wanted to offer you an example of some of the kind of reflection I also undertook to discover what I cared most about. By now, you also know how my mission to build Grant Blvd is rooted in my larger life story. But the soil where I decided to plant Grant Blvd and my other ventures are embedded in many ways, in a different, very specific context. For the last twenty years I have made my home in the Greater Philadelphia area, the birthplace of our nation. It has also been a city burdened by the sad distinction of being the poorest large city in North America. Forty-three percent of our city's urban population is Black. Fewer than three percent of businesses in Philly are owned by Black folk. Only a tiny fraction of those Black owners are women. Many of those are "solo entrepreneurs" running businesses so small they have no full-time employees. This entire context was central to the hard lessons that I had to learn about where I had correctly identified my target consumer AND how I had failed to really understand their needs. What I learned is that this is an error you can recover from, but it's also one that can be avoided. Now you know what I didn't- if your product doesn't meet a clear demand, if it doesn't seek to actually outpace that demand, you'll end up in the red.

Add in the fact that all businesses of any kind need capital to launch, learn, grow, and survive. Ninety-seven percent of venture capital is managed (i.e., controlled) by White men. It's virtually impossible to gain access to funding, especially for the small-business person, and even more especially for women of color. In addition to cash, you also need social capital. Who is in your network? Chances are you're like me: your sphere is narrow and not cash rich. What's more, time is another precious, essential resource. But for women, the responsibility of caring for others places a serious drain on our energy, or time capital. Realistically I, like the majority of women, started from an incredibly challenging positioning as an aspiring small businesswoman. So how did I answer the three "whys" of entrepreneurs?

## Questions Only You Can Answer

Once I came to see the terrible damage of incarceration and then also peeled back the glamorous layers of fashion to see the human exploitation and environmental catastrophe it was built on, it seemed like there should be a way to address both problems in one business. Why not take on both a social justice problem and an environmental problem by taking a radically different approach to making and selling clothing?

*Why is it important now and to whom?*

It's been important for a long time, but there has not been enough energy and attention dedicated to fixing it. My observations came before George Floyd and the Black Lives Matter movement. Before Greta Thunberg and the youth movement demanding climate action. Before the Covid-19 pandemic brought normal life to a halt and gave us space to question what mattered. But these various social upheavals were right on time to generate wider awareness. When my intuition told me to make a way, I began to move, even though a broader awakening hadn't happened yet. One moment that has shaped my drive was my first visit to a men's correctional facility in 2018. Although I had spent years studying mass incarceration and listening in deference to folks who had been incarcerated, being inside a men's maximum-security prison was, to put it succinctly, disturbing. To enter is to be stripped, in ways, of your own sense of freedom. I went inside with a six-person delegation of leaders and Pennsylvania State Representatives. We were there to deliver an uplifting message of encouragement to the entire inmate population about our collaborative work to ease the struggle of reentry. But in truth, the visit was a bitter one. We spent time in a breakout conversation with thirty-five juvenile lifers about their insights, and what they told us affirmed how much more harm than good the prison industrial complex is guilty of.

I started Grant Blvd because I realized the many insidious ways in which their convictions denied the formerly incarcer-ated—especially women—access to living-wage jobs. Being shut out from meaningful opportunity creates the economic/

recidivism crisis. I wanted to create jobs that made a better life possible.

*Why am I the right/best person to build it?*

For the first two years this was a challenging question for me to answer with confidence. As someone who didn't go to fashion school or business school, I often felt like an imposter early on. I was never even a kid who read fashion magazines. But one thing that had always been true was that from a young age, I believed that I was called to alleviate some form of suffering. Teaching wasn't going to be the only lane I operated in. As I looked for another route to be of service, I did an assessment of what I thought I knew. Beyond that, Grant Blvd is the block I grew up on but more deeply, it holds the story of two American families: a family who knew stability, security, and hope—which, until I was thirteen, was us—but it's also the story of a collapsed family, of adulthood depression, of self-medication with cocaine and religion, of weighing "criminal options" as a means of coping and surviving. Grant Blvd is the place where I learned the power of acting with love and of speaking out against inequity. It defines at my core who I am.

In addition, I had grown up with a sense of style. I inherited textile knowledge from watching my mom and from my father I held a deep appreciation for telling stories and tending to things I loved. I also had all that time with my dad in our lovingly tended backyard garden on Grant Boulevard, and hours of learning to value nature and its seasons. These formative experiences gave me my first loyalty: respecting the natural world. I didn't want to build or do something that degraded the environment. The question that arose for me was, "What if I filtered approaches to fashion design through the lens of sustainability?"

When I looked at things that way, the pieces seemed to make total sense to me. I had qualifications! And once I saw it, I never would have been able to consider any other way. What I didn't know then was just how high a hurdle it was going to be to disrupt hundreds of years of industry practice and consumer ignorance. But then again, can't you say the same about every big decision you've ever made? How could you possibly know how it was going to turn out? If you had somehow known *exactly* what was going to happen, would you have been energized to set things in motion?

It's easier to say "life is a journey, not a destination" than it is to live that philosophy because living it requires you to choose to act regardless of the pressing emotions caused by uncertainty. But you can't be an entrepreneur without having the faith, stamina, and determination it takes to start down a long, winding, unmarked road and stay on it.

## The Disrupter

When I looked behind the perceived glamour of fashion, what I saw was a system built on the abuse of people and the degradation of natural resources in ways that continue to contribute to the social injustice and the environmental catastrophe we're all witnessing. The amount of textiles from discarded clothing clogging landfills is staggering. In the U.S. alone, twenty-one billion pounds of textiles end up in landfills every year. That's equivalent to *every* U.S. citizen throwing out seventy pounds of apparel annually. And that number is growing exponentially. [4]

Faced with deeply entrenched capitalist systems and colonialist supply chains that generate billions of dollars in

---

[4] University of CO

revenues and profits, getting into the fashion game as it's currently played wasn't an option for me. "Disruption" had to be my entry strategy. "Disruption" describes a process whereby a smaller company with fewer resources is able to—if they're savvy, nimble, creative, lucky, and committed—successfully challenge established incumbent businesses. Specifically, as larger, more well-known brands and corporations focus on improving their products and services for their most demanding and most profitable customers, they often end up ignoring the needs of other potential or smaller customers. Newcomers (YOU!) can create market disruption by strategically targeting those overlooked consumers. Appealing to this underserved or undervalued customer base can provide a foothold in the marketplace if you are able to deliver attractive, better-functioning products that align with the passionately held values of this target group.

Typically, this theory of disruption shows up in businesses challenging new or emerging markets. Uber challenged the conventional taxi business, then Lyft, who attempted to lure Uber customers. Whole Foods began offering higher-quality organic food options in the grocery sector in sharp contrast to traditional grocery chains. In the fashion space, the clothing brand Everlane positioned itself as offering sustainable garments to appeal to shifting consumer values seeking more sustainably sourced clothing and greater pricing transparency.

Each of these startup companies found an opening (called a "white space") that the established businesses were ignoring or incompletely satisfying. These "disrupters" built their business and brand specifically with that perceived spatial market opening in mind. But to be clear, most businesses who aspire to market disruption have repeatedly demonstrated a willingness to accept the exploitation or abuse of people and natural resources. Even the disrupters have too often been unable or unwilling to challenge the way the business at large fundamentally operates at each step in its process of creating goods or services. And that's most certainly *not* the kind of disruption or innovation I wanted to pursue. The disruption I aimed for had to value *all* aspects of the business—protecting and supporting a "triple bottom line" of people, planet, and profit. How? By remaining true to my own sense of purpose.

As I began to define Grant Blvd and my vision for its long-term viability, I took a close look at the fashion industry in general, but specifically I needed to understand the operations of emerging "progressive" companies that were making claims of "sustainability." What do they claim to do? What do they do well? What are they failing to do that I can factor into my approach to a service or product that their current or future customers may be drawn to? And how do I do that **boldly**?

What would I have to create to attract this audience? How could I offer them something that aligns with my purpose AND demonstrates how a business can take care of people and the planet? From this altitude, how can I build a business that genuinely meets the practical and ethical needs of customers? These are the questions that helped me frame a strategy to reach an initial market with hopes that early success would ripple out to reach larger markets, always with both product excellence and triple-bottom-line impact in mind.

Innovative disruption theory gave me a framework for understanding things business leaders need to consider:

- *Disruption is a process.*
- *Disrupters offer something unique.*
- *Disrupters define success differently ... and not all efforts at disruption are met with success.*
- *Disruption requires strategic partnerships.*
- *Disruption requires struggle.*
- *Disruption requires artful iteration*

## About the Process

Most every innovation—disruptive or not—begins life as a small-scale experiment. Disrupters tend to focus on getting the business model just right—the way they operate as an enterprise rather than merely perfecting the product. Think about how Uber made getting a ride vastly different from hailing a cab. When the experiment shows promise and the business model seems to hold together, the innovator moves from the fringes of a new market closer to the mainstream. Established businesses will begin to take note of a threat. As the disrupter begins to siphon off existing customers or bring new customers into the industry, over time, as big-business market shares and profitability show signs of decline, their leaders may feel pressure for their strategy to evolve. An entire industry may begin to change its established practices, absorbing and even mainstreaming practices that were once operating only at the fringe.

This process takes a significant amount of time and, honestly, carries great risk. Most startups fail not because they have a weak idea, but because they don't have the capital to outlast the long game of pushing back against the big players.

As the founder of small companies, I personally know this to be true. The challenges under-capitalization pose can't be emphasized enough. Companies with brands that have been in the game for a long time can get incredibly creative in the defense of their established franchises, market share, and customers. Their efforts all aim to crush the competition. It takes a lot of experimentation with almost every part of a business model—from how you approach marketing budgets and methods, to product design, to how you decide on packaging—to get it right. Experimenting and failure is costly. However, if you're not experimenting, if you're not taking calculated risks and regularly placing small bets, you can't disrupt the market where you seek to thrive. But you absolutely *can* survive long enough to thrive if you can plan for and finance playing a long game.

Remember, building a business is an act of creative strategy, yes, but it is also one of emotional, intellectual, and physical endurance.

## Unique Offerings

Sometimes disrupters build businesses that fill gaps in the current marketplace. Sometimes they build unique businesses that have never existed before. This takes courage. How do you know it can be done when no one has ever done it? Being a pioneer requires intense amounts of commitment. Even worse, it can be very lonely. Before I started Grant Blvd, I searched for a community, however small, of other business owners, freelance creatives, and nonprofit organizations equally interested in the challenges of this kind of professional (and personal) adventure.

Finding allies and, more importantly, who I affectionately call my "accomplices" (people willing to make sacrifices in support of my success) has brought and continues to bring tremendous value to me. This has come in a variety of forms. Some accomplices were willing to share their networks by making "warm introductions." These introductions were typically made via email but were done in a way that described me and my work with a deep sense of admiration and trust. In these moments, accomplices shared (or, in other words, risked) their social capital to help connect me with someone who they thought might help my projects make progress. Other acts of accomplice solidarity have taken the form of grant- or loan-making—times when people who controlled deeper pools of monetary capital leveraged their cash resources by making an interest-free, unrestricted contribution to the work I was doing. At every stage of the journey, it's necessary to be receptive to and grateful for those willing to invest their social capital and/or financial capital in your work.

## Success for the Disrupter

My goal has been to venture into deeper thinking about the potential of business and to elevate my aspirations to create a business that is an agent of change. But deep thinking and lofty ideals don't guarantee that any concept will work. I had to acknowledge that there are lots of reasons why good ideas, or even what appeared to be great ideas, fail. One traditional way of thinking I had to let go of was how we as a society define failure and how we measure success. I have come to believe that only you can determine what each of these looks and feels like. How will you define failure in your efforts? What metrics will you use to determine if you've achieved success? These are questions that need to be asked for each product you design, each event you host, and each fundraising effort you make. What's more, they ultimately have to be defined by you as the business leader. Once you have that clarity, you can empower your team to recognize success specific to the roles they play because together we move the entire organization forward. Forward is the motion we focus on.

What I can tell you from the research I've done and the experiences I've had as a serial business owner is that we can be successful at disruption beginning with what we conceptually imagine, what we design, and what we aspire to. Sometimes, meaningful disruptive innovation results in six or seven figures in annual revenue, revenue that can be invested in growth, in scaling. But sometimes business ideas, simply because of their courageous innovative nature, can fall far short of your original intent, and that's okay. Why? Because there are learnings in all losses. What, for example, did you learn in the process? How can you apply those learnings to build a more robust business? *Hear me when I tell you:- failure is not disgrace.* At least it's not if you commit to learning and growing from it.

In fact, there is a special kind of knowledge that comes from being able to both look backward *and* forward, from futuristic imagining. Nothing taught me this more than watching my brands grow in public visibility. We saw an increase in our social media followers and our public relations opportunities, but we did not see that translate into actual sales. The optics said that we were doing fine, better than fine, but in reality there were years during the pandemic when we were scraping by, trying to avoid taking on ridiculous amounts of debt. Yes, there was a massive jump right after the murder of George Floyd, but most Black-owned businesses saw that energy dissipate within eight weeks of that moment of racial reckoning. Yet, I continued to hold on to my intuition that I had to keep courting customers. People don't see something once or twice, or even three times, and then buy in. Conversion takes patience. The path to profitability requires not only strategic genius, but Olympic-level endurance.

## Strategic Partnerships

Because so many of our current systems and supply chains are oppressive in deeply ingrained ways, it's essential to identify who you believe would be strong, reliable, mission-aligned strategic partners for your venture. I looked for other service providers, particularly those who were "hyperlocal," or what I define as within an hour-and-a-half drive from where we produced and sold our goods. I needed partners who could support my team. I went looking for other business owners whose communities and networks were open to "cross pollination" through mutual marketing and promotion. They had to be businesses who truly believed that "a rising tide lifts all boats."

What I found was that building the strongest base for strategic partnerships should include businesses both inside *and* outside my fashion sector. For example, while we absolutely partnered with photographers, makeup artists, and fashion stylists, we also needed to partner with companies that shared our values. These range from local bakeries (shoutout to the bakers of Beyonce's birthday cakes: Cake Life), to innovative producers of items outside our product category, like the W Hotel (of the Marriott hotel organization), and the Philadelphia Union, a professional soccer team. This was helpful in two key ways: cross-promotional campaigns with these partners grew our reach, and it also affirmed our brand's commitments. An added benefit was that I could learn from leaders in other industries by watching how they solved problems similar to my own but seen through a different lens.

## The Struggle

To build bold businesses, we have to accept that we will face struggles. And that struggle will be very, very real, particularly for those of us who are daring. For some of us, our struggle will be compounded by our ethnic identity, by our gender expressions, by our sexual preferences, or by the limitations of our bodies. But we must never lose sight of something Frederick Douglass called out nearly a hundred years ago when reflecting on and challenging exploitative systems: "If there is no struggle, there is no progress." (West India Emancipation speech, 1857)

What I see around me in business, in politics, in relationships is that *progress moves at the speed of trust.* As folks dreaming of or already building bold businesses, one of our most significant challenges is around fostering trust. We have to fight for our visions, fight on behalf of the changes we aim for our enterprises to address, and fight to stay clear about our ethics. It's a fight because our supply chains, local policies, and normalized practices tempt us to cut corners and ignore harm. And what this moment needs from us right now, what it needs from you, is your commitment to joining business leaders who are at the frontline of what has to be the new way going forward.

Our natural world is on the precipice of irreparable, catastrophic damage. A legacy still linked to gross abuse and systems of slavery internationally is being protected to meet our collective need for instant gratification and for what feels convenient. That in mind, what part of your business model can you experiment with more boldly than ever before in the spirit of breaking things up in your industry or sector? How can you be more strategic about the small bets that you make next? Moving forward, and this is a challenging question, how will you define success? How will you measure it in the short term and the long term? How will you actually track your progress?

What led me to start a business is the belief in its power for innovative disruption. The intentionally designed triple-bottom-line business sees a gap, builds to fill that gap, and offers a service or product that challenges toxic systemic patterns. That's what businesses like Grant Blvd aspire to do with clarity and integrity:  to create meaningful, visible systems change. That's what your business can and must aspire to do, too.

## Submitting Receipts: What is a B Corp?

At the foundation of every intentionally built business are the things that matter most to you as the founder—your core values. Values are not tangible things. Values are these nebulous, floating, abstract ideals that ultimately guide and motivate us. For too many of us, our core values have always been expressed in money and acquisition. But when I think about the state of our criminal system, when I think about the state of our planet, it becomes painfully clear how striving for wealth, how hoarding and a scarcity mentality have been responsible for shaping deeply problematic, inherently toxic decision-making on the personal, regional, national, and even global level. Setting money up as the key metric and end goal is not sustainable for the planet, and it's not sustainable for your soul.

As I've mentioned, starting and building a business—especially for women and even more so for women of color—is a lonely pursuit. And if you don't want to be another "business as usual" enterprise, it feels like you're entering an unknown, even hostile environment. When I found myself in that space, I started searching for the comfort of some kind of community.

If you need proof that you never know where connection and inspiration come from, here's another instance. I first saw the B Corp™ logo in Target. When I checked it out, I knew at once it totally aligned with my ethos. I met B Corp™ on the shelves of a mainstream marketplace, and it was a game-changer. Here was a powerful organization that was clearly defining social entrepreneurship. They had done the most concrete work in setting up a rigorous set of standards for businesses who want to be and do better. As I learned more about the B Lab certification process, I believed that at the very DNA level of Grant Blvd, we were already acting like a B corp.

I didn't know what we still needed to prove, but as soon as I found the B Corp community it was like stepping into the waters of a warm, reassuring, powerful stream whose force came from a strong, ever-expanding network of social entrepreneurs. I didn't just put a toe in—I dove in. After a year's worth of challenging, dedicated time to complete the assessment and application process, Grant Blvd became the first Black-woman-owned B Corp™ certified business in the fashion space in North America.

A lot of internal work, a lot of introspection, and a lot of changes in me as a leader had to happen first. But it was absolutely worth it.

## Making a Difference with Beer

An example of a B Corp leader near and dear to me is my friend and "accomplice" Tess Hart, co-founder of Triple Bottom Brewing in Philadelphia, the first craft brewer in America to receive the B Corp certification.

Triple Bottom launched in 2019 and was less than a year old when the pandemic shut down the country. Tess's story, from business design, to launch, to early pivot and scrappy survival, illustrates much of what I've been describing about the struggles of social impact entrepreneurship. Together with her husband Bill Popwell and business partner/brew master Kyle Carney, Tess set out to build a craft brewing business that was distinctly different from the industry standard in both visible and invisible ways. The craft brewing industry is dominated by White men, but Tess's workforce is fifty percent people of color and fifty percent women. All breweries consume a lot of resources, but Triple Bottom works hard to manage their consumption responsibly, tracking water, gas, and electricity usage and setting goals to reduce resource use.

All of their electricity is from wind power—most of which is produced in Pennsylvania.

None of this has been easy or quick to accomplish. Tess spent nearly four years researching the elements that would enable her to achieve her mission of being a "fair chance" business with a strong company culture in which "people respected each other's differences, lifted up the good in everyone, learned a lot, and had a great time being together." (www.triplebottombrewing.com). "Fair chance" for them means offering meaningful, living-wage jobs for people who have experienced homelessness, incarceration, or other barriers excluding them from the mainstream economy. Tess built relationships of trust and mutual support, what she refers to as an "ecosystem of advisors," with a variety of organizations to learn about trauma-informed care, the work of local social justice leaders, and the needs of neighbors who lived near the brewery. The goal was to create a genuinely welcoming business that celebrated and uplifted their community through delicious beer and intentional collaborations.

Prior to launching Triple Bottom, Tess had experience working with foundations, social enterprises, government, and nonprofits. Drawing on all of this professional knowledge, she wanted her business to operate from a set of values that led to joy and connection, empowering each other to craft a better future, and protecting the health of the planet. As Tess describes Triple Bottom, the company's DNA means making every decision based on supporting their community and the environment—not just their profit margins. Her "triple bottom line is beer, people, planet." (www.triplebottombrewing.com)

Even the most thoughtfully laid plans are not immune from catastrophe. For Triple Bottom, as for so many other small businesses, the pandemic caused derailment. Tess had just made her final construction payment, depleting the business bank account. When Covid-19 suddenly shut down the city, there was no revenue coming in and no expectation of when it might return. Tess furloughed her team so everyone could collect unemployment. She made a major decision to invest in a mobile canning line so their beer could be transported. And she reached out to a network of other small producers who collaborated on a lifeline for their local businesses: a "Joy Box" of home-delivered artisanal, small-batch treats including ice cream, chocolates, coffee, cheese, mushrooms, and beer.

Reflecting on the lessons of the pandemic, Tess felt it showed how adaptive and resilient we can be while holding on to our core values. Her hope as the business continues to grow post-pandemic is that Triple Bottom will inspire other entrepreneurs to challenge the unjust, exclusionary, or destructive practices that have become industry standards. She believes that we've shown we can all adapt when we have to. Now is the time *to choose to adopt new ways of working* by building businesses that serve the greater good for all people through inclusive workplaces, fair wages, and responsible management of resources. Triple Bottom Brewing is a beautiful, real example of this ethos in practice.

## The Value of Belonging

Thinking back on the long and exhausting assessment process Grant Blvd went through, I believe the B Lab self-assessment process is the best place to start when you begin sketching the design of your organization. Completing the B Lab impact assessment represents a sizable investment of time and resources. For fledgling Grant Blvd, it took us over a year of effort. But going through the process helped me examine what I was building, figure out where there was room to grow, and how to move toward. The effect on me as a new CEO was powerful. It got me to see things I had not been taught to see. B Lab showed me how to move as a leader—it showed me that *all* of my decisions have to support the same core values consistently and clearly, from what cleaning supplies we purchase to who we bring on as employees.

This unified way of values-based thinking is not standard business school material. Becoming a genuinely values-centered business required a lot of rethinking, a great deal of communicating, and a whole lot of coaching to get people to do things differently—to move away from their usual methods and materials and learn a better way. To be effective as a CEO, you've got to embrace being a teacher. Luckily for me, I was comfortable taking on that role. I was asking my employees, suppliers, and investors to pay more attention to the details, just as I had asked my students to do in the classroom. I had to learn to articulate what we were doing, envision what more we could be doing, and share this with my team and others. I was beginning to practice strategic communication, an approach that proved helpful in my first round of raising capital.

Acceptance into the global community of B Corp enterprises like Patagonia put us in the class of brands and their thought leaders who had built successful businesses dedicated to supporting the welfare of people and planet with profit, and beyond that, with a sense of clear purpose. Investors want to see some proof that your concepts are validated and that you understand what you're talking about. Earning the status of B Corp provides a known, shared language. It signals our dedication, our expertise, and our leadership.

My hope is that it will position us to leverage what we've built so far to get what we need to continue to grow. While that has not yet happened, our standing as a B Corp helps to validate what skeptics might view as our far-out notions of equity, inclusion, social justice, and environmental stewardship as cornerstones of our for-profit business. I want to stand with companies who aspire to a higher level of nobility. That's an act of solidarity that means a lot to me. It is the only place I want the companies I build and advise, to land.

## Key Takeaways:

- **Truly knowing who you are and why your business idea matters are essential first steps to entrepreneurship.**
- **Define success in ways that are meaningful to you and your own sense of purpose.**
- **There is no disgrace in failure, only in failing to learn and to continue to iterate.**
- **Forge partnerships of trust within and outside of your industry.**

# CHAPTER SIX
## Curating Your Team

Despite the inflated claims of far too many prominent entrepreneurs, nobody makes it to the top on their own. Somehow, however, that American bootstrap mythology of the scrappy businessperson who rose from obscurity to fortune and fame persists, though I think there are some signs that it's loosening its grip on the popular imagination. The simple truth is that nobody, and I mean nobody, achieves their highest goals or full personal potential without what I affectionately recognize as the support of allies, accomplices, and mentors.

My kind, curious parents always believed deeply in the enduring value and transformative power of education and community. You might remember how much loving attention went into the dress my mother made for my fifth-grade graduation. But by the time I was graduating from high school, my family had completely disintegrated. If I wanted some pomp and circumstance, I was going to have to make my own plans.

I'd been making my own decisions and pretty much managing my young life solo by then, so pulling together a graduation celebration for myself felt like the only option. In a time before email and social media, I did what I could to put out the word to anyone and everyone I thought might show up to celebrate my achievement. With what little cash I could spare, I cobbled together some snacks and beverages back at my house on Grant Boulevard and waited nervously for guests to arrive. As was the case with my sisters, our mother never appeared at my graduation or at my graduation party. My father, no longer able to present in the ways he once had, came in at the very end of the window without much fanfare. There were no phone calls from relatives that week, no excuses or apologies or explanations as to why no one was coming. In fact, only two of the people I had invited came and on that day, they were the only people who lovingly sat in community with me. It was a crushing experience that I have never recovered from. The memory of which sits further complicated by the truth that one of my two guests took her own life just a few years later.

This context is important. To this day, I hate throwing events of any kind or issuing any type of personal or professional invitation. Whenever any of the companies I lead host events it's hard not to be triggered into a panic that no one will show. But I keep doing it, I keep putting myself out there as a hostess and reluctant event planner, because I've learned that emotional resilience is another type of muscle. You have to exercise it even when you're not feeling it or it will quickly atrophy. And if you don't keep putting out an invitation for people to show up for you, you can definitely rest assured that no one ever will.

## Finding & Feeding Community

My high school graduation provided me with a powerful insight that has shaped the way I look for help. A true community is not something you just walk into. It comes from doing the hard, risky work of seeking the people who are willing to pursue a mutuality of availability and connection with you.

You have to be vulnerable enough to let them get close. It comes from doing the hard work of aspiring to see yourself as enough just as you are and calling on that self-acceptance to fight rising feelings that you are insufficient, that you are inherently unprepared. And you are, I am certain of it, capable of pursuing this internal work. Perhaps this feels familiar to you, and perhaps it doesn't. Regardless, when we start thinking about where to get help, we tend to focus on the people we are closest to. For some, that may be a fertile place to look, but it's not inherently guaranteed that your greatest support can or will be found in your family of origin or the neighborhood you grew up in. It certainly wasn't the case for me. But this reveals the power and art of curation. Curation is defined as "the action or process of selecting, organizing, and looking after the items in a collection". We have the power to recognize and decide who will choose to count on.

Women in particular tend to think we have to do it alone. As a result of modern culture there is (for good reason) so much fear that things aren't safe, that people aren't safe, that if we don't just do whatever "it" is, nothing will get done. What's more, many women have endured significant emotional trauma inflicted by people taking advantage of them. It's undeniable that a deep vein of misogyny runs through global culture, one that perpetually gets fed in many places by systemic racism. As a form of protection, we tend to insulate ourselves—how to hide, how to shrink, how to wilt. We've been led to believe we are inherently insufficient because we're women. If we seek help it's a sign of submission, or worse yet, neediness. Admitting to being "without" has been dangerous for us—it's forced us to sacrifice our time, our dreams, and for some of us, our bodies. This thinking is certainly also true for men, though the conditioning at times may involve a peculiar set of messages that needing or wanting help is a sign of weakness and fragility.

As businesspeople and as human beings, the things we build can't just be raised or tended to by us. If your business requires you to be part of it *all the time*, it can't grow and what's worse yet, you'll burn yourself down to the ground trying to be everything it needs. This level of intense engagement may make you feel in control, but it also significantly limits what you can accomplish. We have to surrender over and over again to the support of other people who we intuitively trust have our interests at heart, to people who we believe want to see us win. Sometimes they can show up and sometimes they can't. In my experience, it's those who actually show up, even in the case of my tiny graduation party, who matter most.

## How to Know What You Need

Before you start looking around for who you want in your corner, do some careful soul-searching about what you actually need. Do what you can to get specific. The more specific you are, the more successful you'll be at uncovering what will be most useful to you now. I've made the mistake of not ordering my needs and that meant I didn't order my asks—I didn't know how to. As a result, I got things (people, resources, support) I wasn't actually well-positioned to deploy effectively or efficiently. And because I couldn't use them appropriately, I either underutilized them or lost them altogether. Make that mistake once or twice and you'll see how costly it is because you can't go back to those same sources for future help.

This process has to begin with self-awareness and absolute honesty. I encourage you to begin here:

- What do you have and what are you missing?
- What's the best way to prioritize your needs in the short term?

- What do you do well and what do you do less well or maybe not well at all?
- Can you humbly acknowledge that other people can do things you can't do or do them better than you can at least at this time?

Being strategic is always keeping top of mind an awareness of where things are and where you want things to be. You should be alert to what other people bring and how it may help you move forward. It's not a superficial transaction. It's like the video game Tetris. It's looking for alignment, not extraction; seeking mutual benefit, not misuse.

One effective way I've found to determine alignment is by asking people what they're excited about at the moment. That's a subtly but importantly different question than asking "What do you do?" What I've discovered is that if their excitement and mine align, we can make some magic happen. That said, I'll never forget the very last time I ever asked someone to "pick their brain." I was about to be honored by *Black Enterprise*, who had named me the "Business Disrupter of 2022," a huge national award. I was in the lobby of the convention center when I fell into easy conversation with another nominee, Derrick Hayes, owner of the franchise Dave's Cheesesteaks. At some point I casually said, "I'd love to pick your brain sometime." I was impressed with the business empire he was building in the food space and wanted to learn more about how he was reading the national landscape. He was gentle, but he made it very clear that that wasn't the way to proceed. He said, "What if we build together? I don't want to have my brain picked." Powerful, right? I was reminded that afternoon of the importance of aspiring to build with people—not to just, even if accidentally, extract from them.

In my constant effort to extend and strengthen my community, I've been clear (and persistent) about both accepting *and* rejecting notions of age, race, and gender as limiting factors. I believe that if a person is twenty-one years old, they probably have a temperature check on culture that would open new possibilities for my brands. If someone is sixty or older, chances are they've already learned something I have yet to experience. Their lived experience might enable them to be more efficient and productive, and for sure they will tell me if the wheel I'm struggling to invent already exists.

Recent political campaigns have made me aware of who I think the genuine change agents are. They're the ones who can communicate a vision and build a richly diverse coalition in support of it. I admire the leaders in politics or business who can bring radically different people together into a culture or organization in a way that seems both safe and welcoming. A place where each individual's uniqueness has value. As a business leader, you build such a coalition by knowing what you need to fill your niche. The missing elements transcend race, and don't rule out the queer people and the straight, the rich and the poor, the young and the no-longer young. Community is about knowing who to invite in and recognizing that even within a subset of human beings, there is deep diversity. To build a collaborative team that sets you up to succeed, everyone has to feel authentically cool as who they are when they come to be with you. My experience has shown that when you create a culture in which people from the margins participate fully without a sense of shame or apology, deep loyalty results.

## Creating Capital: Knowledge and Funding

So, what were my gaps as I started planning and dreaming my business into being? A big one was the most obvious:

experiential knowledge. I had never run a business of any kind. I had never even interned in a business. I had no legitimate business experience, no academic degree like an MBA, and I knew nothing about marketing. Beyond that, I didn't even know how to network—as a classroom teacher those were, on the surface, unnecessary skills. I didn't come from inherited wisdom about running a business. My parents' deli closed its doors for a number of complicated reasons they never talked with me about in any detail. Admittedly, my lexicon for business is still developing, and initially, my lack of command of the shared knowledge of business insiders made people think I knew even less than I knew. I was coming to entrepreneurship as an outsider, bringing with me an outsider's lens focused on doing things unconventionally.

When confronted by the unknown, I always revert to my trusted playbook: education. I already had a Ph.D and didn't think another degree would serve me, so I opted against pursuing an MBA. Instead, I used my own money and took a class in the business of fashion at Made Institute, founded and run by a woman named Rachel whose values seemed similar to mine. I wanted to jump right into the capstone course in the curriculum. Rachel gently but firmly walked me back from my aggressive approach. With her insight and coaching, I learned how to put together a credible business plan. That gave me space and a template to conceptualize what I wanted to achieve and why. Working on the plan helped me map a way forward. It gave me a widely accepted framework for sharing a vision of who I was as a businessperson. These aspects of professionalism and credibility really matter. Without them, it's too easy to sound like just another naïve wannabe business owner, the sort we are all suspicious of when they tell us about their "business ideas" because most "great ideas" simply don't succeed on their own.

But besides this, I began to reframe what I *did* know. After having worked as an educator for over twenty years, I reflect on my experiences and take into account the organizational, communication, and social skills that this career has afforded me. Each day I entered my room, my sanctuary, unsure of how my well-laid plans would be received. That experience taught me the importance of flexibility and innovation. Being a classroom teacher taught me how to command a room of up to fifty people—teenagers no less—how to put on a costume, how to navigate staging, how to deliver a monologue like I'd never done before. These are essentially the skills that I learned how to raise hundreds of thousands of dollars, to give keynotes in front of hundreds of people, and ultimately, to grow my influence. I bring all this up to say, we all have levels and layers of latent skill. It's up to us to decide how we can reframe each chapter of our personal and professional experiences, and ultimately, talents.

Part of my early-stage research was trying to find some funding sources that seemed open to startup ideas like mine. It started when I Googled "crowdfunding." I wanted to see what options were out there and how other people had found financial backing. When I read about a new fundraising platform, IFundWomen, I channeled my efforts into positioning my business plan to their specs. I was betting on them and when they accepted me on their site, they were betting on me. The folks at IFundWomen were really excited about helping me figure out how to inspire crowd-sourced financial investment. Their guidance gave me the crucial insights early-stage entrepreneurs need to hear and to learn how to raise money by telling a compelling story about their plan.

IFundWomen gave me a platform for asking strangers for investment. But once I had a solid business plan, I reached out to many of the people who already knew me: my neighbors in the community, my fellow teachers, my college friends. I literally told everyone I could think of, regardless of their net worth, "This is what I am doing. Can you help?" Making this direct ask of people you know is much harder than it seems. It's not so much about the money as it is about the exposure. You have come out publicly and announced your intention to everyone you know. Now your idea takes on a whole new reality. It goes from being something you are secretly thinking about to something you have said you are most definitely going to do. That raises the stakes considerably. Suddenly, you are accountable to just about everyone you know. If you've ever set yourself a goal, like losing weight or learning Spanish or getting back into dating after a bad breakup, you know how having accountability can be a heavyweight. But it can also be a jetpack motivator. I say go public with your fledgling business idea. Be courageous enough to give people the opportunity to ignore you, give you some capital, ask a question. If you are open, each person's response can trigger what happens next.

## Community, Identity, and Communication

Creating a growing community is about who you already know, or the folks you make the effort to meet who can connect you with their people. By reaching out to the widest circle I could touch, I got the first capital I needed to build a business and open a studio space. This process of seeking early financial support enabled me to be connected not just to my core of early believers but to their connections as well. Think of this process of enlarging your community as strengthening the lungs of your personal ecosystem. A supportive community provides the oxygen that fuels the cells, the veins, the muscles that create movement. At any point in this ecosystem, you will encounter someone who can give you some advice, a bit of money, or help you to understand the goofy language of venture capital.

Building genuine community is about understanding that creating and maintaining relationships is a reciprocal effort. No matter where you are on your business journey, you need to make space to witness someone else's journey. Witnessing can happen long-distance from across the country or in person. It might happen in times of triumph and in times of trial. Holding space for other people to reimagine themselves is the same space you want to be given. You win more when you invest in rooting for other people. That channel of energy you send out might be returned to you when you do your next hard thing and need some extra push.

If it were easy to do this, we'd all have stronger networks of support. But there are deep-seated cultural norms that get in our way. The first is the pervasive belief in scarcity. Time, money, energy, faith, empathy, and compassion—we are told we need to hoard these for our own protection against disaster. We are taught to be brutally selfish as our main tactic of self-preservation. Something or someone is always out to crush us. I don't believe this.

Being in genuine community with other folks means being consistent with everybody. In the company of a shoeless person or a celebrity in Blahniks, I work to give everyone the same energy. To treat everyone with dignity because I never know what they can offer me or what I can offer them. The person who asks me for a dollar might be the one who changes me. It doesn't make sense to me to view everyone as my competition. I don't feel afraid of big or small things whether it's someone stealing my business idea or seeing my hairstyle and wearing it. It won't ever be the way I execute on it or wear it. People are open-source creations—people want to adopt. I'm going to do it my way and they will do it theirs. My way is going to be solid, so I don't even care about imitation. Once I've moved into a space where I want to act, I don't see people as a threat or competitor. I see them as my equals. They're not heroes or villains. They have talents I don't have. It requires a lot of humility to navigate this notion of how we are building and holding relationships in community. We have to practice believing in what's possible together instead of what we're afraid of losing.

Along with our anxiety about scarcity is a fear of honesty about confessing just how hard things are. Fake it till you make it, right? In a culture like this, how are we to show up as our real selves? After all, who are we? I've always found that especially challenging as a Black woman, so I understand why people feel they need to manage this closet of masks. Social messaging both coaches and confuses us about the "right way" to present—if you're poor or didn't go to college, for instance. There are any number of traits that make you "other." We're taught we have to be selective about how we present ourselves to different audiences if we want to be accepted. It's exhausting to take a bunch of masks on and off, always trying to anticipate what every group of people expect or want us to be. Our bodies are not meant to pull off a quick switch (what we recognize now as a "code switch") to sync with a wide variety of identities. The truth is we are all multiple things. We are moms and divorcees, daughters, and creatives. I am all of these things at once and you are, too. Owning our complexity is human. It demands to be recognized. All that dancing around, that shucking and jiving many of us have conditioned ourselves to do, exhausts energy in places that do not serve the direction you should be moving toward. If you can find ease and comfort by accepting all that you are, you put yourself in a position of strength instead of apologetic weakness. Until that happens, you will struggle needlessly. When you don't have power, you can't command power. I don't even want to lift my hand to change a mask, and I'm surely not paying storage fees on a collection of masks.

Ultimately I've learned to accept that it's actually less burdensome to instead hold space for all our identities at one time. I encourage you, therefore, to allow yourself to accept yourself fully and in doing so, to be many things at one time. And here's why: the truth is that you *are* many things at one time.

## Say No to 24/7

Time is undeniably a limited resource for all of us. In fact, it is, in that way, our greatest commodity. There are only so many hours in a day, days in a week, weeks in a month. And we never can know how many years will be ours to experience. Maybe as a way to push back against time constraints, we have become a culture addicted to being busy. The way I see it, this notion of busyness is filling your life with things to do without considering if they are helping you to be productive or successful. I'm not *busy*. I'm not a workaholic. I'm being productive. I'm sober, ten toes down, in my one precious life.

It's true that I live by my calendar. It is one way that I maintain discipline and a sense of order when it comes to my time, but what gets on my calendar is not automatic. Until you can afford a personal assistant (virtual or otherwise) or a chief of staff, you have to be your own gatekeeper. Before you commit your time to something, ask yourself, "What are the long-term objectives and what has to happen day-to-day to achieve that?" I'm treating my time as precious, spending it hour by hour, or limited to thirty minute intervals. I used to think a thirty minute meeting was an affectation people put on to show how high demand for their time was. Now I've come to recognize how much can happen in half an hour if that's all the time you have available. Ask yourself how you are valuing your time and value it appropriately. Ultimately, your calendar shows what you care about the most and your time is your most precious resource.

That said, being available can make the difference in relationships, and vibrant relationships undeniably contribute to a happier, healthier, longer life. Making time for and creating space for other people to do the same for you might seem "unproductive," but it adds immeasurable value. As we think about how we spend our time, try reimagining how we can be better to other people in an effort to keep them in our lives. What I've learned is the power of intentionality: the more I've learned to be judicious, the more other people have come to understand the value of my time, and I theirs.

This is not a 24/7 practice, and it is not without learning how to set and communicate boundaries. Everybody can't come into your life; everybody won't be able to have direct and immediate access to you. Sometimes what they bring is not good for you, and sometimes what they offer might work against your best interests. And there are going to be some who don't want to come. Sometimes, people are not even invited to the party and that is okay. Time management is about preserving and holding sacred what you need. It's about identifying what's urgent and establishing what must be prioritized. It's about how you want to invest your time.

My life as an entrepreneur/mother/teacher/leader is physically and creatively demanding because I aspire to achieve bold visions. This has required incredible time management, discipline, and sacrifice. But I haven't chosen to lead a movement in entrepreneurship because I want to be busy or gain more visibility. In my view, the "booked and busy" game is an ego game—when you play it, you're not focused on the things you need to be focused on, because it forces you to lose sight of your priorities. In other words, you stop being led by what you need to be led by. Instead, you get drawn into a performance of being deemed influential or important. That approach easily becomes a lifestyle fueled by a desire to get social approval, but it's a losing game; it creates exhaustion and misery. Living this way will wear you out from the inside out—it will drain you and it will absolutely age you.

Instead, I hope we can see our value and live it out accordingly. How? Draw lines around the time you can give. Decide whose opinions you truly respect. Ultimately, getting comfortable with setting limits comes with emotional maturity. Be able to firmly act as though your time is not a menu for others to choose from. Be clear about what you are willing to give fully. Being honest about calculating what your value-add is in any situation increases your value. I often ask myself when I'm deciding what invitation to accept, "Will being there strategically move things forward for me?" Or, of equal importance, "Will it add to my own sense of joy and success?" The less you feel compelled to undervalue yourself or spend time doing things that don't align with who you are, the sooner a sense of greater control and accomplishment will replace the "crazy-busy" life so many of us choose to live because social media told us to.

## People Positive

One new threat dominating the headlines is the explosive growth of artificial intelligence. As I think about AI's potential impact for changing the landscape of work, it seems to me our best defense is our humanity. Humans will always be drawn to optimism and technology can't replace that. Instead of scheming to secure your place, aspire to be a sincere anchor of optimism. Trying always to come from a place of persistent gratitude for life and its potential has served me very well. As a public-facing businessperson, I've learned how much power is in a smile. A real, with-your-eyes smile is not weakness or awkwardness—in some cultures it's even an act of charity. It is a sign of your full presence and your willingness to acknowledge someone else. Community is recognizing when someone is receiving what you have to offer and demonstrating a capacity to be available for you. And it is also carving out space to be available for others.

It may sound easy, but it's hard as hell until a mindset shift occurs. Our own individual traumas and our toxic culture combine to prevent meaningful integration of people, beliefs, and values. There is so much resistance to making that happen. Yet I believe it is when people figure out how to come together for their common good that the magic happens and that we each get better aligned.

One of the things that makes me most proud of Grant Blvd (and Blk Ivy Thrift as well) is that we keep holding on despite every challenge we face every single day—whenever we held public events like a collection launch or staged a pop-up shop for another small business in our local community, the diverse faces in the room reflected what I've tried so hard to cultivate. There wasn't always a clear, visible majority group. Instead, there was a consistent spirit that felt like the experiment of America just may be meeting its potential.

## Key Takeaways:

- **It's okay if everyone doesn't show up. Focus your gratitude on who does.**
- **No matter who claims otherwise, no one succeeds on their own or all the time.**

- The energy to consistently execute also comes from cultivating a diverse coalition of supporters and watching them enjoy the fruits of your labor.
- Invest in yourself and protect your most precious asset: your physical, mental, and emotional health.
- Hold on to and offer pragmatic optimism- it's an irresistible energy.

# CHAPTER SEVEN
## Surfing the Wave

From the absolute very beginning, our survival has always depended on our ability to pivot. When I say, "our survival," I'm referring to not only my business ventures, but also to myself personally. I've survived because I've been pivoting all my life. So has the human race at large. This is our story. But just because we've always had to do it doesn't make doing it any easier or any more fun.

At times, deciding to pivot might suggest going in a whole new and different direction. It might require that you go back to your why and completely recalculate. But I believe the power of the pivot comes from staying the course you set for yourself, from always staying in close relationship with your personal due north. Each time I set out to achieve a goal, I've come to accept that it may mean I have to jump over a high hurdle or break through a high ceiling. I've come to understand that simply moving in the direction of a vision I have requires some surfing, that it might require me to swim figuratively across a wide stretch of choppy open water, unaware of what I'll have to face. And this has never stopped scaring me entirely. Instead, my trust in myself, in the general arc my journey will take, has grown.

In your process of moving through business ideation, execution, or even your life outside of your role as business leader, you're responding to the inevitable fact that the landscape changes day by day. If you're going to make it, and I mean long-term, measurable success, you have to adopt a mindset of being agile while trying not to resist or ignore the obstacles. This means committing to surrendering everything that you cannot control, and that's more than it's comfortable to admit. Try to stay loose in your body and mind so you can let things go, accepting that you can't control the outcomes. If you can make this choice every day—and it is a choice you must make every day—you'll be able to free your energy up to accurately see your priorities and to pursue timely solutions.

But all that acceptance and letting go doesn't mean you should allow yourself to passively drift wherever the uncontrollable elements are pushing you. Trying to avoid falling into the path of least resistance may give you a temporary sense of relief, and trust me, finding relief from the pressure you might be feeling is necessary. But surrendering without a strategy will likely mean you lose all of your enthusiasm. I've learned that not facing hard things is a dangerous game to play with poor returns. Instead, it's been helpful for me to develop what I like to call "intellectual agility." This agility of mind has enabled me to problem-solve more efficiently. Most importantly, it has freed me from the emotional burden of feeling ... stuck. Here's the thing few people will say: seeing the fear and anxiety that you're inevitably feeling and then consciously choosing to see beyond it lets you step up to the 30,000-foot-view level of your environment and your circumstance. Intellectual agility allows you to see what is and see it more clearly. By using this skill, you can better scan the far horizon—your big-picture goal—then think clearly about what might be the best path forward. It helps you to manage your emotions and be your own true compass. This practice also works to increase your "courage quotient" as I like to call it, or your capacity to take risks in public. Your business survival requires that you cultivate this ability. And for your business to go beyond survival, to arrive at the hard-earned feeling of thriving, you've got to be able to stay focused on the long view and the long game. By cultivating intellectual and creative agility as a business leader, I've become much better at making sense of complex information and to reorient my operations proactively and reactively in real time. Creative agility is how my team and I keep coming up with solutions that keep us headed in the direction of our values. Intellectual agility helps me know how to lead us all.

## Sometimes Your "Great Ideas" are All Basically Wrong

This is more or less the theoretical description of the process I've inwardly developed, but I learned this framework on a practical level when I first launched Grant Blvd. In the beginning of the journey to build that brand, I made just about every classic mistake business novices make. Much of what I thought I knew, most of what I assumed about my target audience, was quickly revealed to be flat-out off. We were designing products driven by our values: tackling climate change, centering social injustice, offering living wages, tending to the fallout from mass incarceration, and offering an alternative to the unethical and unsustainable practices of the global fashion industry. All the best things, right?

When you put all these efforts together, the clear target market would be GenZ. The data all points to this conclusion as a sound one. But for Grant Blvd, it quickly became painfully and expensively obvious that I had miscalculated. In reality, despite their value statements the younger consumer is still self-medicating an addiction to fast fashion. Grant Blvd was mimicking trends and stepping ahead of them frequently, but at a higher price point than mass producers. Younger consumers could get those styles or similar ones from big-box brands who couldn't care less about their social or environmental concerns. It turns out, my imagined target audience did not have the emotional will or perhaps the budget to choose goods built on higher values offered at a higher price point. What's more, my initial target consumer was in this way a "conscious consumer", or a consumer looking to shop and live, sustainably. Well, you know what's most sustainable? Not consuming much at all. I had made a major miscalculation.

A second key element I missed was that most conversations about sustainability almost exclusively engaged White audiences. Because I am Black, I assumed Black women would immediately and enthusiastically be my most loyal customers, and in a city that is forty-three percent Black, they were also what we call in business my "closest dollar." But sustainability design so far has been a conversation mostly directed at and participated in by White folks and my pseudoscience on identity politics was missing the marketing budget it needed to land in front of this particular other audience. By failing to recognize the limited reach and acceptance of sustainability principles, I'd already lost half the population because the message I was making was never able to reach them. Instead, the middle-aged White women who were already buying products produced in alignment with their progressive values never fully connected with our design aesthetic as it endeavored to appeal to the young and to people of color. This, as you can assume, created missed opportunities and stunted our growth.

These challenges were compounded by other factors we had very little control over. I hope understanding lessons like this show you how any well-intentioned but misguided action can put strains on your entire operation. Specifically, mistakes and missteps eat away at your revenue potential, your operating budget, and your capacity. In these early days of discovery, we were riding as I like to call it, "the struggle bus." However, we had to learn from these miscalculations and learn to execute on intentional pivots, fast.

As if that weren't enough, we signed our first lease for a retail space in January of 2020. Two months later, right as we prepared to open, the world shutdown as the Covid-19 pandemic circled the globe. We had to cancel the photo shoot we planned which was central to our initial product launch. The models we'd recruited for the shoot had all scattered in search of physical safety and at the mandate of local leadership. Did we throw in the proverbial towel and give up? No. I did something incredibly uncomfortable. I asked my then preteen daughter to use my cell phone and together we cobbled together a photoshoot using our still empty retail space. My daughter served as stylist and our Director of Design acted as photographer. With little choice I stepped in as the only modeling talent. Ahead of our opening our team had worked so hard to meet our production goals, and we applied the same intensity to moving forward. That first release nearly sold out in a matter of weeks.

Then, in acceptance with the dire state of the situation locally, we made the quick pivot from selling women's fashion to cutting, sewing, and selling face masks. With the city in a state of lockdown suddenly we had to pre-cut and deliver fabric kits to our sewers' homes. We asked them to make cotton masks instead of women's clothes so that they were able to stay employed despite the crisis and so that we had something relevant to offer our consumers.

## Recovering from Missteps

As a business leader, how do you respond to the things you don't know how to do? I tried to ask questions from everyone

I thought could help, starting with my internal team. I was willing to try new things and grow my own abilities, even if that meant becoming something wholly unfamiliar, like standing in as a fashion model. The fact is I couldn't afford to hire someone who already knew how to do the myriad things I was inexperienced in. I could ask people questions and I could try to emulate their flow. I could study what I was seeing in other leaders and other business models and try to adapt it to my situation. I could make quick, strategic decisions. I had always been a great student, so I went in search of learning. Taking on that burden of being "chief solutions officer" is what being a leader requires of people like us who are taking on the unknown.

That's how we operated until we could hire more experienced people. But even then, I was still required to spend each day acting as both student and teacher. During this early time, I especially leaned into my team for advice and focused on identifying their diverse talents. We had so many discussions that opened with "What do you think is the best way?" We all had to embrace being in a state of near-constant experimentation, which is admittedly hard. Through this process of seeking, I learned the wisdom of trying not to invest too much in the testing, even though limiting the extent/cost of the experiment means you're not running the best test possible because you can't afford it. You do what you can reasonably and responsibly pull off. Otherwise, you burn through your emotional, creative, and social capital in ways that are unproductive.

It was critical in the earliest years, and it still is, that as an organization we all remained true to our original values and vision. We had to resist the strong pull to sell out, and we had to protect our culture of care—care for each other, care for our consumers, and care for our wider community.

Our shared commitment to a transparent set of values helped hold us together and keep us motivated.

A main way we defend and protect our values is by being transparent. On the wall in the Grant Blvd store is a graphic explaining how we arrive at our retail prices. The cost formula puts specifics behind our process so that customers can see where the value is in their purchases. On an annual basis, we as an organization decide what we can do for others and what we can give away. This information forms our annual business impact report and offers proof of how we are prioritizing and achieving the type of impact we aim for. Honesty forms the foundation of the business. It starts with your leadership and a commitment to genuinely sharing the story of what you are doing and the how and why behind your business practices.

However, product design was one extremely challenging consideration because it involved so many tough decisions. It still does. Let's look at the selection of fabrics, for example. In an industry so comfortable with dishonesty and exploitation, we had to find our lane. We had to try to solve the perpetually crippling crisis of not being able to find sustainable, ethically produced fabrics. One way we hit on was to offer the truth about the source of our fabrics and their contents. If we're going to use denim, how do we offer some that is at least one hundred percent made in America? If there is polyester in the garment, how do we educate our customers about the pros and cons of this petroleum-based material? How could we do a better job of assessing and providing what customers say they want? We had to take all of these risks by formulating and testing our best guesses in the harsh reality of the marketplace. This included asking the most important questions for any entrepreneur: does this product appeal to our audience?

Does it solve a problem? Can we tap into demand? Is this a price they are willing to pay?

## Pivoting Is A Practice

There were other pivots we needed to make. As a small company, how were we to address size and gender inclusivity? Were we supposed to? Did that approach benefit our business model? Did we only want to dress women? We thought we were losing an entire demographic of people who might want to support us, but we had nothing to offer them. What could we do for men? How would we cut and design for this untapped market? As a customer-facing company, we continue to challenge ourselves about how we are responding to who we *think* our audience is. As a result, we are constantly checking our assumptions against who they actually are.

When we first started, we used the models that I knew—people who were twenty, twenty-two years old. These young women were supposed to tell the story of our audience. Now, I had to include an older demographic to indicate that I knew who I was talking to and who I actually needed to be talking to. Since I was no longer twenty years old, it made more sense that I figured out how to address the demographic of my people: progressive professional women between the ages of twenty-four and fifty-four. These were women who shared our brand values and were ready/able to shift the investment of their disposable income to shop with us. From our initial youth-themed fashion designs, we pivoted to contemporary office wear, and the sorts of pieces this audience might put on for art museum openings, date nights, and special social occasions. Clothes that are practical to this chapter of life without sacrificing color, style, and statement. That was a pivot that has proved very helpful to us.

I spent a lot of time looking at other clothing brands who appeared to be making a lot more money. I came to see with more and more clarity that their profits were made on the backs of exploited people. They sourced whatever materials earned the biggest returns, and produced at such aggressive speeds that they had become responsible for the hundreds of tons of clothing clogging landfills all around the world. Inherently, I knew that this way of producing a profit was wrong. It has for many years been obvious that we need a new class of entrepreneurs, daring leaders able to use business as a tool for resistance and reimagination. Grant Blvd's collections in this way are offering a new model. They were an acknowledgement of the fashion industry's ties to the legacies of American slavery and the millions of people who shed tears and sweat to produce bales of cotton. In this way, we maintained clarity of position and our promise to our customers: we were different.

## Pick Your Battles

I realize this may not be the fight you want to fight. I imagine some of you are not manufacturers and probably don't aspire to be. But at the very least, I urge you to know who your manufacturers are and to build more partnerships with smaller producers. Go beyond knowing them to demand transparency in your relationships with manufacturers. We have to be more judicious about who we are willing to do business with, or we will never bring about change.

Again, little about this is easy. My ambition is to give you a framework for seeing the shifts that need to happen more clearly. There are strong headwinds of market pushback against change. There always have been. We're dealing with increasing social tensions, anxieties about the economy, more frequent and severe climate catastrophes, and new uncertainties posed by the quick adoption of AI. I admit that the success of companies who disregard the negative impacts of their businesses on people and on the planet have discouraged me at times. Our company mantra is "forward is the motion." Believing in this is how we keep ourselves inspired as we continue to search for the way forward. Right now, that means experimenting with more pivots.

We anticipate scaling up by developing a new "B2B" product line designed to meet the clothing needs of restaurants and hospitality businesses who promote sustainable and ethical practices. Through such partnerships, we could add a new revenue stream, diversify our customer base, and have a much greater impact as employers.

My larger goal is to grow large enough to be in a position to demand changes in the ethics of our global supply chain. We can't know what the outcome will be of the work we do. Ideally, more than wealth or fame, the contribution of my leadership may be changing the conversation somewhere else. Maybe in Germany or Nigeria, people will become more committed to embracing a more just way. Maybe somewhere in Asia, producers and consumers will be brought into deeper awareness that fashion could be approached as a force for social benefit. Maybe it will inspire one billion business owners to evolve into social entrepreneurs.

As business leaders responsible for people's jobs and livelihood we're all clear that securing profits in the short term is absolutely necessary. It's undeniable that taking care of overhead requires both capital and revenue. But in the longer view, our aspiration as daring visionaries must be to make things better for humanity globally by changing what we accept in each of our industries. History offers us examples of leaders who were not businesspeople but whose ideals brought about changes in the workplace and in society—people like Gandhi,

Dr. King, and these days, social-justice-minded advocates like Michelle Obama and Malala Yousafzai.

I've accepted that this process of evolving and pivoting never ends. Staying in business is a tumultuous rollercoaster. In that way it reflects the nature of work and of life. Framing change as a constant sets us up to go the distance. In light of the fact that the overwhelming majority of small businesses fail within three years, and even the viable ones struggle to make a profit in fewer than five years, you've got to commit to going the distance. No one affirms that the landscape is treacherous and uneven, that the sun is hot, and that when you've been slogging through a desert, even a small success feels like you've arrived at the oasis.

I always focus on paying close attention to the wins, reminding my team and myself when we get a cool press feature or have a great meeting with exciting new potential partners. Even though most of the promo photographs we take in any given shoot are useless, we work to orient our gaze in the direction of the win: each time we've ended up with a dozen that are undeniably magazine-quality. So much of success in business is about the cultivation and preservation of this mindset. Other people aren't going to point out the wins for you along the way; you have to see them and celebrate them for yourself and for your people.

## Character Comes First

Succeeding is so much about expectations, learning, and making adjustments. Starting Grant Blvd was not my first experience with naïveté and lack of exposure that caused me to seriously underestimate what achieving my specific goal would demand. When I enrolled in a PhD program, I firmly believed that getting the degree was all about taking classes.

So, I signed up for a bunch of them and carried a heavy load to accelerate the process. Turns out, as anyone who has gone after a PhD knows, about sixty percent of the work is in the classroom. Then, there's the staggering forty percent still ahead: the dreaded dissertation. Here's when so many can't hack it and end up settling for the facetious "ABD," all but the dissertation. My mistake came so naturally. After all, I had never known anyone other than my professors who had a PhD. No role models, no peers, no one to speak frankly with me to tell me what to prepare for or expect.

Going into business was the same deal. We can't ever really know what we're signing up for. Maybe if we did, we might not do it. But couldn't you say the same thing about so many other paths you've gone down or decisions you've made in your life so far? None of us are gifted (or cursed) with the ability to accurately predict the future. Committing to business means moving into a journey that is iterative—experiment, analyze the data, decide if it's a win or a loss. In HR, PR, hiring, firing, budgeting, product design, operations, marketing—in all of that, we are learning and trying to figure out how to become better. Better at experimenting and better at collecting and interpreting the data. Better at determining what it points to as a next step. As a teacher I learned to be reflective in my classroom practice, and I bring that same approach to my business. That's what we should all expect from our leaders in every aspect of their actions, whether it's fundraising, pitching, hiring, or planning for growth.

Character is what we're talking about. What does that even mean? It's our ability to stand in a place of integrity while holding in our awareness the cacophony of needs within a complex system that are not explicitly only our own. Our workers, our consumers, our community, our planet all have pressing needs. Character is embodying a mindfulness of care. This doesn't mean you are a pushover. As anyone who knows me will attest, I will negotiate to the day I'm dying. I am very clear in asking for what I want, and I remain reluctant to accept what is not fair. You can do that and still act with character. This is a way of being. It develops over time and with life experience, based on what you've been exposed to, read, suffered through, and survived. Character is about endurance. Character is earned.

It seems to me we've lost touch with the beauty of character, a way of conducting ourselves in public and private that contributes to being admired and trusted, to truly being a leader. We've been conditioned to wait for someone to save us or to come in and lead us instead of stepping up ourselves. This reluctance to step into advocating for what is right shows up in small and large offices, in restaurant kitchens, and in male-dominated corporate boardrooms. This hesitancy also does not serve us.

I've come to view business as part of a longer human story. The first ocean sailors in the South Pacific came to understand how to use the stars to navigate. They spent much of their voyages traveling in the dark, yet they made it to shore. They learned how to be comfortable being in the dark, how to surrender to the journey. That's a major, undervalued skill and one that savvy entrepreneurs have to train themselves to do. We need to develop an ability to navigate in the dark, guided not by stars but by character, unwavering values, and the due north worth following.

## Key Takeaways:

- **Change is inevitable, so your ability to pivot nimbly is crucial.**
- **Recognize your biases (we all have them) and work to adjust your lens.**

- Your due north has to be your steady, guiding direction. If you lose sight of it, you'll lose sight of your vision and what it requires.
- Take note of and celebrate the wins, no matter how small. They're your fuel.

# CHAPTER EIGHT
## Embrace Your Story, Then, Share It

As a daring leader you've begun investing your energies into building a company based on your values and your vision. Part of the big-picture work of being a social entrepreneur is actually about how well you're able to convey the significance of your business to both familiar and new audiences. This is crucial. Without deep self-awareness and self-acceptance, it's not really possible to express effectively who you are and why you are doing what you're doing, a process central to good storytelling. It's also not possible to sustain any fabricated story—having to preserve an "alternate" character is a lot of work and most certainly not worth the effort.

The story you tell about who you are—your what, why, and how—has to be what you care to cultivate. It has to be consistent without being boring. It has to be compelling without being dramatic. Especially when so much customer outreach happens on social media, people expect to be entertained, but they don't want to feel coerced. They want their learning to be engaging and fun. In short, they want a whole lot. You might even say they want too damn much. But it is what it is. To be a social entrepreneur is to accept this charge.

Being a social entrepreneur is being many things at the same time, and one of those inescapable roles is that of storyteller.

Humans have always communicated through stories. We can trace this practice back to the oral tradition of the global ancients who came together around a fire or who gathered out in the open air to listen to and be carried away by a story. The best stories may move backward in time or into the future, but the goal is always the same: to help us make sense of the current moment and to help us navigate it.

Stories drew me into a lifelong habit of reading and into teaching. My time as a high school English teacher helped me develop as a storyteller in so many ways. Standing in front of a classroom of teenagers, you learn to be a very skilled performer, comfortable being onstage, delivering the same lines over and over as if you never said them before. You understand costuming and its power to send a message about your personality. You learn how to be in touch with the whole room, the importance of eye contact and proximity. You learn to read body language and to modulate your tone. Effective storytelling is about looking at the room, virtual or real, and seeing/sensing how the audience feels. It's about capturing their attention and holding it. In today's social-media-obsessed culture, that too often means having to manage the operations of your business *and* finding the energy to literally dance on camera to promote your brand. It's a lot.

## Messaging and Measuring Impact

CEOs all serve as brand ambassadors, especially in the early stages of the company. We have to be able to hone our ability to perform for various audiences without faking it. The best actors know it only works when they take a temperature check on how they are being received. The sudden gasp, the burst of laughter tells them that what they're putting down is being picked up; the knowing nod indicates when someone personally identifies with something you've shared. Acknowledging your audience and adjusting your delivery to get the crowd reaction you want is all second-nature to a skilled storyteller.

Often our contact with our target audience will be virtual so we won't be able to see their reactions. Instead, we will study a range of data analytics, pay attention to press coverage (when we're lucky enough to get it), and monitor mentions of our brand to assess how people are receiving us. For me it has meant questioning if I was able to successfully take people on a journey that led them to support (and by that I mean become consumers of) whatever a particular venture was selling. Even now I constantly ask myself: have I carefully established *who* the characters are in this story, *what* they long for, *where* they are going, and *why* my audience needs to join them? I know that if I can do that, if I can get my target consumer to "buy in", holding their attention gets easier. Being attuned to how your message is being received helps you know when to acknowledge shortfalls and adjust your delivery. In other words, it sets you up to strategically and successfully make shifts.

Before you start changing it up, however, pause and evaluate what metrics you are using to gauge the effectiveness of your outreach. Top-line sales and how they convert to bottom-line profit has to figure significantly as a means of measuring success. Sure, you want to drive traffic to your website, and you want this traffic to convert to sales. A suggestion here is to of course use data analytics to better understand your site and other digital tools to observe the level of engagement across the platforms that you use. Tracking tools like these can be helpful to guide your decisions about timing when it comes to your content. But these measures can be discouraging and are not always able to tell the full story of what's working or why. Ask yourself if you are communicating a story that goes beyond promoting items for sale and tells how what you are doing has real value when it comes to the core needs of your target consumer. Are you effectively telling your viewers the value of supporting you as it relates to them? Your messaging has to do more than rack up "likes" for the simple reason that "likes" don't pay the bills. People may say they admire you from afar, but if that admiration doesn't translate into conversion, specifically into repeat purchases, it can destroy your brand and sink your business. If you're not getting the conversions you need, don't initially take it as evidence that your product design is failing or that your offering is inherently without value. Instead, let it also serve as a signal that a messaging pivot is likely required and so might be an increase in your marketing spend.

The challenge to be precise in our communication is one that every business owner faces. How can your messaging build enough momentum that demand outpaces supply? How do you develop your ability to release your unique power, influencing people and culture in a way that is accessible, digestible, and enjoyable in ways that sound and feel like you? You may not always be the best judge of this. When I'm on social media posting to promote or share something, I don't think it sounds like me at all. It's not disingenuous, it's just not a voice I recognize as mine. But the people who know me well say it sounds just like me and for my community, that matters.

So much of being comfortable in your identity as a human being is becoming able to fully express who you are and what you stand for so that you can find and speak to your people. That is the great work of being a social entrepreneur. Consumer psychology research tells us why people buy what they buy, how they identify their needs, and get their needs met.

While I'm not going to explore this emerging science here, it's one worth studying. As a brand ambassador you need to understand what your "tribe" wants. You have to anticipate it so that what you produce in message, products, and services has the potential to attract them to you, even if they didn't consciously know they wanted to be near you.

Although the immediacy and intimacy of social media hasn't been around that long, appealing to customers' emotions has a deep tradition. Revlon didn't become a huge success by selling lipstick. They sold specific emotions—the desire to feel beautiful, confident, and desirable. Amazon sells convenience. McDonald's sells nostalgia. Everyone with a product or service is selling to human beings with feelings. Successful brand ambassadors know how to acknowledge and meet the emotional needs of their target market. Finding the right language, the right message, the right tone to reach your target consumer comes back around to being comfortable in your own unique identity as a human being and in your capacity to connect with the identities you share with this, your audience.

## Who is Your Ideal Audience?

As you're hunting for a sale, do you know what animal you're tracking? How do you find your tribe? For me it was by trial and error, like throwing spaghetti at the wall to see what sticks. You begin by casting a light so your tribe can find you. Not everybody is going to see you right away. Don't swallow that as a sign of personal failure. It can be cancerous to take this personally. Instead, make adjustments and keep trying.

First, you will find your group of committed supporters among your friends. And in the process, you will discover new friends while uncovering who aren't in fact your friends. Your locus of support rests among people who share your concerns. Realizing who my target market *wasn't* helped me align my finite energy with people who naturally shared my vision and values. The better you can align your target consumer with who you are, the more effective you will be.

When I first launched Grant Blvd, I was basing my/our brand identity on sustainability. But what I soon discovered was that White folks had largely created and owned the sustainable conversation. The Black and Brown audiences I wanted to reach were not using that language of "reuse, recycle, repurpose," nor were they in an economic position to think about the future in those terms. Sustainability was a conversation for an elite group with the means to think far ahead. As a result, I was unintentionally talking to a narrow set of people—essentially, progressive, older White women. That's not who I initially intended our base to be, but it proved to be the group that responded most enthusiastically and immediately to my messaging. As a result, I came to see that the channels of outreach and voice I was using did not need to change, but the content did.

For starters, our images needed adjusting. A picture truly is worth a thousand words. We had to change our models—add more diversity, include older women, and feature different body types. Being differently inclusive shifted our focus, enabling us to better align with our initial supporters without compromising our core values.

It's my belief that Black women have always been powerful leaders of American culture—behind the scenes of what we're wearing are Black women who determine fashion trends. These undervalued women were the ones I wanted to talk to. These were the women whose respect and admiration I wanted to earn by designing clothing expressly for them. But in the beginning, that wasn't happening.

## Finding the Motivating Message

When the idea for Blk Ivy Thrift came along, launching pushed me into the spotlight and affection of people of color in a new way. This new venture grew out of the deep impressions left on me at an early age by cultural influencers, primarily the writers and thinkers of the Civil Rights Movement. These were the people I wanted to be. Maybe surprisingly, given its inspiration in the protest movement, the tone of Blk Ivy Thrift feels curated and warm.

The response was nearly immediate. Launching Blk Ivy Thrift was not a conscious effort to create an historical context for Black women in America. I saw it as another avenue for resisting business as usual, aligning us with a larger community of activists beyond fashion or commerce.

As it were, it took a new product approach and brand identity to reach a new audience. This particular audience shared my politics and concerns, and they responded to how we made an effort to openly talk about what it's like to be a person of color in America by highlighting issues related to the fight for civil rights. The sense of connection they felt to the brand's focus earned their trust and gave them comfort. It also opened up a channel for our team to introduce them to Grant Blvd and its value proposition. Both brands were able to cross-promote each other and to help me gain influence as a leader among Black, Brown, and progressive White women.

Ultimately, the full expression of my understanding and values were always captured by both brands. Having two companies with different primary audiences had power beyond marketing. Since a key goal for my business is driving change, having a diverse coalition of supporters has always been critical. Lasting progress has only ever been achieved by a diverse coalition of people at the base of the movement. I therefore see these two brands as representative of a continuum of the kind of social and environmental change I believe in and the impact I want to have. Together, they affirm that you cannot be a faceless, valueless brand in the era of social media. The cultural climate will not, over time, reward the absence of a relatable leader.

The danger you face when you try to expand your audience is the pitfall of trying to be everything to all people. My businesses can only be all of the things I authentically embody. This is why I often reflect back on my guiding identities. For me, it is immutable that I show up as a Black woman, as a teacher, and as a mother. What are your immutable identities? The bottom line is getting to what you cannot repress about yourself simply because it is true, and leading from there. Next, find the safe people to share those identities. The sustainable life as an entrepreneur happens when you've built a community of people who celebrate your immutable identities. Customers show up for you as you want to be seen. That creates a vibe for consumers. You offer them a product that aligns with their shared identities as caring people. People are drawn to others who embrace their own immutable identity and enable everyone to express their own, too. People want to be in an inclusive and authentic community *with* you.

Showing up to tell your story is absolutely of the utmost importance for an entrepreneur, especially those trying to make important changes in the world. But no one tells fledgling entrepreneurs how to find their true self. At some place on this journey, you need to think about your internal landscape. It's impossible to communicate a story you can't see. In my journey, there were two helpful practices for talking about the hard things that hold us back: therapy and private meditation. We do ourselves a disservice while trying to discover our authentic self if we don't trust the power of therapeutic support and solo meditation. We all need to find the resources that can assist us as we try to understand how to see ourselves.

Part of seeing ourselves is rooted in seeing other people and in reflecting on how they/their choices have affected us. In deciding to name my first company after the block I grew up on, I didn't initially realize what that meant I'd have to face. And not just once—it would be a story that I'd have to tell repeatedly. I had to tell it honestly, and that meant disclosing truths that for a very long time were painful for me. A beauty of that choice that I discovered in hindsight was that it propelled my own journey to self-discovery and healing.

I had to share complicated truths about people I care about, namely my parents. I've learned that navigating autobiographical storytelling demands more than just the pursuit of truth. It also demands the pursuit of tenderness.

In order to achieve this, I've found these principles of ethical storytelling helpful:

1. Tell your own story, speak the truth, and stay true to your own facts.
2. Accept that other people may not agree with your version of what happened.
3. Share your plan to be public privately and directly first.
4. Seek consent as a way of demonstrating your integrity.
5. Offer grace and humility when revealing what might cause others to feel a sense of shame or embarrassment.
6. Be authentic.
7. Be tender with yourself and with the stories of others.

My intention in sharing what was both true and tragic about my childhood was never to punish my parents. It was never to make them feel guilty or to humiliate them. I felt a sense of responsibility to speak with care about them and to take accountability for my framing. My goal was to share with compassion what their choices were, my understanding of those choices, and how those choices affected me. It was also to honor and to protect. Your story is yours, but where causing damage can be prevented, I'd like to encourage you to pursue that path. In doing so, you may bring about even healthier, more restorative outcomes for not only yourself and the work you aspire to do, but for others.

So far in this chapter, the discussion has been about the way entrepreneurs tell their story to their audience of potential customers. But there is another important audience business founders and leaders need to speak to: the people who control the money. Investors, lenders, granters have different needs than your customers. Learning to communicate authentically and powerfully with these groups is a separate skill. In the next chapter, I'm going to share some of what I've learned in my business leadership journey as I've looked for and found the capital necessary to establish and grow my businesses.

## Key Takeaways:

- **Communicating authenticity is a superpower.**
- **Engaging, true stories offer your audience a way to experience your product.**
- **Your brands embody who you are and what you value. This is legacy work.**
- **Be honest but speak with tenderness.**

# CHAPTER NINE
## Cracking the Money Code

Before I committed to starting Grant Blvd, I had mostly managed to avoid having to ask other people for money. Working all kinds of jobs as a teenager, applying for and winning scholarships for college and graduate school, signing on for low-interest student loans, supplementing those funds with teaching gigs, and being conscientiously frugal were how I stayed afloat. Then, once I found a solid full-time teaching position, I committed to living very, very far below my means so that I could keep my debt low. I bought used cars, spent every dollar available through my employer to pay for graduate classes, and mostly thrifted. Peace of mind was always having some "extra" cash in the bank. Confidence came from knowing I could take care of and count on myself. And that approach freed me from ever having to stress about money (a rare privilege, I know). Instead, I was able to invest my income into spending weekends away from my small apartment and enjoy traveling to twenty-four countries in ten years.

Culturally, many people see being in debt as natural, normal, completely expected, and necessary. That was not my position. In my adolescent years, I had learned to survive—barely—without having cash on hand. No surprise I developed a lot of anxiety about the idea of being in debt. As I got really serious about growing Grant Blvd, I knew that I would need a pool of money to help us stay afloat and enable us to take some calculated risks. Years of careful saving and thoughtful spending still did not add up to the amount of capital even a modest startup requires. Early in the planning stages, I realized raising money had to happen. Soon after that, it became apparent that business debt was going to be unavoidable. Without sufficient capital the business would die on the vine. It's not necessarily bad ideas or poor execution that lead to failure for small businesses. Too often, it's simply running out of runway, which means running out of cash. I had to do a personal, emotional pivot and push through my anxiety about debt.

Then, I had to figure out who to ask for money and how to actually make the "ask." This was another stage in my evolution as an entrepreneur. It was another example of working out what it meant to be willing to learn by doing, and it led to even more instances of "throwing spaghetti on the wall." When I think back on this emotional transition (and that's what it was: our relationship with money is often emotional), I want to say there were basically two things that I didn't understand about raising money. But that's a major understatement. Even now, years in, I am still figuring the practice out. Finding funding is an incredibly dynamic, complex, even obscure and mysterious process. So, let's start with the first two things I learned that have proven to be true.

- People invest in leaders with compelling visions.
- Your vision has to translate into a product or service that you can package and sell over and over again.

## You Are Your Most Valuable Asset

More than the business plan you've worked so hard on, how you come across to potential lenders or investors determines whether they will be moved to hand over some money. The expression you sometimes hear is that "investors are betting on the rider, not the horse." Before investing in you, they look for evidence that you can make sound decisions, that you can recruit and retain talent. They also want to find reliable evidence that you have matured into a subject matter expert about your business and its place in the industry. They are watching and listening to decide whether you personally have the goods, the energy to create and maintain the necessary momentum.

Next, there's your vision. Can you convince them that there is a market for what you want to sell? Are you capable of bringing that product to market? Will you be able to pivot if one or more of your assumptions don't prove true? Have you built in some resilience to protect against external things like high unemployment or the economy tanking? Are you able to communicate your plan for growth?

The first hurdle, convincing people of my authenticity and commitment, wasn't as hard for me as the second one about how my vision translates into a viable product. As an experienced teacher, I knew how to engage with diverse audiences and how to present the depth of my expertise. That said, this is where fundraising gets really complicated because different audiences are motivated to buy into different visions. I found this out by working my way through the various channels of capital. You'll see what I mean as I describe my efforts and the results of approaching different channels of people with capital.

## Tailoring Your Pitch

There are actually quite a few sources of capital for entrepreneurs—at least in theory.

- Public crowdfunding
- Friends and family
- Business loans
- Corporate grants
- Private grants
- Government backed grants
- Angel investors

I'm listing them in this order not because this is the order I suggest you pursue them, but because this is the way I began looking for the startup capital I needed. As I began to gain more experience with pitching (asking for money) and confidence, I used that knowledge to pursue larger amounts of money from a wider variety of sources. Being able to develop some expertise in lower-risk situations is a tactic worth imitating if you suffer from the same hesitation and inexperience I brought to finding capital. I also learned the importance of being able to modify my pitch to the specific audience I was in front of, even if it was a virtual one. It's incredibly important to learn how to read a room and how to adjust to align with it. This not only helps communicate that you've done your due diligence but it helps you to bring home the bread.

My initial effort at raising money was through the online platform IFundWomen. I chose them because I believed in the power of storytelling, and I believed that my friends and family would be more likely to give via a platform that aligned with their own values. The name IFundWomen was a pretty direct and clever invitation to let donors know who and what they were signing up for. I also wanted to partner with a platform that was already amplifying founders' stories and had a strategy for supporting founders who had never done a crowdfund before. They turned out to be a good fit and a great partner. They were able to give me concrete help with creating my timelines. They also shared important tips, like why it's important to have your goal privately funded by nearly thirty percent of your total "ask" before it even goes live.

But while the IFundWomen effort netted us some cash, it didn't produce nearly enough to pull off what I wanted to accomplish. So, a year later I moved over to IndieGoGo, hoping to reach a larger audience through what was at the time a more popular, well-established platform. It wasn't an especially strategic move, but it was an intentional effort to experiment with something new, and I hoped to gain some expanded traction because of it.

Beyond the small cash infusion, what was probably most helpful about both of these online crowdsourcing experiences was the platform's support in helping me figure out how to structure a pitch for a general audience, and to a smaller degree, to get in front of a new, national audience. I also discovered that these platforms are most effective when you have a specific, concrete, tangible goal. We used them successfully to raise money to build-out our first design studio, and then to move into our first brick-and-mortar store. These are short-term solutions. On average, we raised $18,000, which was enough to serve as a quick cash infusion and to accomplish in theory what we promised to our backers, but it wasn't enough to quickly nor fully propel the business forward.

Next, I had to move past some embarrassment about having to raise capital by going the traditional route of asking "friends and family" to contribute. My hope was to reach thirty-three percent of the money we needed before going live with Grant Blvd. But, as for so many people of color, my circle of friends and family didn't have enough ready cash to help me hit that target. They were prepared to give love and support in abundance, but giving money was a harder task. Besides, I knew that the labyrinth for me to access capital would statistically include more intricate swamps and channels than it would for a man my age who was White. Despite how demoralizing the numbers were, I persisted undaunted. I just kept pursuing each opportunity I learned about, each grant and each low-interest loan, uninterested in the odds of my success. I kept shooting my shot.

Sometimes I landed a big opportunity by way of funding and sometimes it arrived right on time, like the time in 2020 when Beyonce and her BeyGood foundation pulled up for us. It came out of the blue in ways. Months after I'd forgotten I applied to BeyGood, I logged on one day to review website activity and saw traffic from the web domain www.beyonce.com. It was perplexing. I did more research and looked at their site which is how I discovered that her team had decided to support us with a $10,000 grant. The support from Beyonce was huge. It was wild. The weight of her approval, of her name, is remarkable. She, like Oprah, has the kind of influence that shapes culture and seems to stop time.

Around this time, I started to be more proactive about tapping into my network. I began by setting up meetings with people in new circles around Philadelphia, where we were going to be based. I met people for coffee at shops convenient for them and talked about my vision for not just Grant Blvd, but the city itself. I gained so many priceless allies this way who, in turn, became brand ambassadors. These new supporters were able to make warm introductions on my behalf to their well-resourced and well-networked friends. This was how we got our first business loan.

Atypically, it came from a private foundation, UnTours, who was excited to support me as an individual and my passion for positive change. Founded by an inspiring social entrepreneur, Hal Taussig, UnTours was the nation's very first B Corp, and they continued to affirm their legacy of mission-aligned investment when they bet on Grant Blvd. They were great partners who immediately figured out how to support me. One of the first things they were able to commit to was a very low-interest loan to help me grow our equipment and inventory. But beyond that, they were a safe place for me to talk openly about the challenges I was facing as a Black woman in business who was raising the conversation about ethical decision-making and sustainability. Under the guidance of an incredible mentor of mine, Elizabeth, they went even further: they offered to serve as our fiscal sponsor. She was clear on the need to decolonize wealth, and she refused to gatekeep what might help me. I believe we need to have more of this kind of solidarity—the kind that opens doors, that builds bridges, that creates space for access to capital. Without a doubt, the UnTours Foundation was committed to my vision, and I will forever be grateful for their solidarity.

Not long after UnTours came on board, I began hearing about corporate and private giving. A number of corporations created initiatives in the aftermath of George Floyd's murder, making funds available for small-business owners with social impact goals, especially those aimed at supporting Black communities. I applied for a number of these competitions offering cash prizes, and this proved very helpful in 2021. Grant Blvd won the UPS/*Inc. Magazine* Small Biz Challenge that netted us $25,000 and some business connections we would otherwise never have developed.

What this set of competitions and opportunities showed me was that pitching to people only works when you fully know and are proud of your story. Only then can you hope to skillfully align your pitch with the specific audience you are addressing without compromising your message or altering your true identity. The timing of these events is undeniably remarkable. Grant Blvd.'s mission hit on the emerging national zeitgeist of deep concern for social justice and the environment. I had gained some influence and was clearly building a company with intention, one designed to create impact.

These no-strings-attached funds are great, but they can be time-consuming. The effort of identifying them, figuring out the application specifics, completing the process, going through interviews, and recognizing that not all the efforts are going to be successful isn't sustainable for an under-resourced small business. That said, all in all I was able to raise nearly $370,000 in grants over the course of six years. Ultimately, it was time well spent.

If you don't have time to do thorough research for grants, looking for a business loan through a bank or CDFI (Community Development Financial Institution) is another option. It was the next direction I pursued on the journey to raise capital. As more funders have recognized the need for small-business support, some bank and community lender programs have been created to offer low-interest loans to entrepreneurs, at least lower interest than traditional banks. Low interest is what made taking on loan debt palatable to me. At rates of three percent or even lower, I felt I could "afford" this particular kind of debt because it allowed me to continue to operate without significantly raising my overhead or triggering my cultural trauma around money. This was a form of debt I felt reasonably comfortable adding to my list of personal financial obligations. However, small loans still weren't enough to fully fund my ambitious vision.

## Facing Systemic Barriers

While I had clearly had success with a diversity of fundraising options, bigger pools of capital meant looking into some unexplored avenues. Among them were coming to better understand the world of venture capital and "angel" investors (high-net-worth individuals choosing their own investments with flexibility in their timelines and levels for returns), large foundations, and government programs.

As I began to be better able to articulate my ultimate goal as one of creating social and environmental impact, I knew I had to recast my story to reach people whose interests allowed for providing "patient money" for long-term impact. It wasn't going to be a pitch about a sustainably made women's clothing line. It had to feature my impact goal in order to activate a response from this group of people with money to invest.

This approach to raising capital is fully dependent on who is in your network, which is why it poses such a significant barrier to people who don't come from wealthy communities. For this reason, it's where many entrepreneurs are likely to hit a seemingly impenetrable wall. The fact is that most BIPOC entrepreneurs are outside of this network, one based on college friends, inherited family wealth, resource rich alumni groups, and impressive professional connections. People of color, particularly women of color, lack the contacts who can give us a "warm introduction" to people able to invest in us. The power of warm introductions is equivalent to someone cosigning with you. It's a strong endorsement that opens doors and wallets. All you have to do is look at the way businesses have been built in Silicon Valley to see how the "network" operates. This is made painfully obvious by how infrequently they choose to invest in Black women. However within this ecosystem, this hidden world, there is major investment capital. It is managed by venture groups (groups of investors pooling resources to invest in opportunities with high, fast return, ideally twenty times their original investment), and through angel investors. Despite being an outsider, angel investors and social-impact venture capital groups continue to seem like the most plausible pathway for me as there is a culture of seeking to challenge traditional investment practices which are exclusionary and unethical.

I also thought working with large foundations might be possible because some of them have an expressed interest in sustainability. Even more discreet and hard to access than foundations are the family offices and small private foundations. While there are thousands of these across the country, they work hard to maintain anonymity. They generally do not put out calls for proposals or advertise their giving outside of a limited circle. They prefer to do their own research to identify candidates/enterprises that fit their mission and conduct their own due diligence. Breaking into this circle is almost impossible. But there is so much wealth concentrated in this sector that I felt I had to give it a try. All of my efforts to reach this "hidden" money rested on strategically expanding my network in an attempt to break into the circle.

Raising money is an extremely active commitment, and I have had to accept that pursuing funding means that I am not spending time on other aspects of my business that need my attention. Instead, I was constantly reframing our story. You'll have to do this, too: update your narrative with how you have navigated the necessary pivots, showcase your leadership capacity, and make measurable progress. Put together an engaging pitch deck, home in on realistic revenue projections, frame the partnerships you have developed and are seeking. All of these pieces have to work together to inspire, cajole, and convince your audience to fund you. Because without sufficient, ongoing financial backing, nothing else can happen.

Lately, women have been told lots of supposedly helpful tips about how to avoid "weak language," or how to assert ourselves and take our place in a man's world. There are some compelling reasons *not* to follow this advice. First, if that's not your style, faking it will be painful and disastrous. Authenticity has to lead. And second, as organizational psychologist, Wharton professor, author, and podcaster Adam Grant recently wrote about women trying to imitate men's tough talk, "The problem arises if people perceive them to be forceful, controlling, commanding and outspoken. These are qualities for which men are regularly given a pass, but they put women at risk of being disliked and denied for leadership roles. (Not surprisingly, the backlash is <u>even stronger</u> when a woman is Black.) Instead of being judged just on their performance, they are dinged for their <u>personality</u>. *Overbearing. Too abrasive. Sharp elbows.* "[5] The way you speak to the channels of money—any and all possible sources for financial support—has to demonstrate who you are and how you show up. And you have to discover how to show up as you authentically are. Being inauthentic isn't worth the emotional toll it will take. It's too much emotional work. Instead, be confident, be clear, and be open.

As a small-business owner with growth plans and ambitions, you are always raising money—whether that's a loan, a grant, or some angel investment—because executing your idea always requires capital and you need more money to sit on.

---

[5]     New York Times
      https://www.nytimes.com/2023/07/31/opinion/
      women-language-work.html

## Another Path to Capital

This brings me to a new frontier for my entrepreneur's journey. After remarkable success raising money to support ideation, we were ready to enter into the arena of government grant programs. To fund a centerpiece of my vision for systems change, we were awarded an economic development grant of $250,000. This was a long journey and meant that while few could see it, I was working diligently for five years to find the right nonprofit partner for a grand workforce-development initiative. That meant hours, days, weeks, and months talking to, convincing, sharing my vision with a wide range of non-profits, never knowing how it was all going to come together. Then, finally, it clicked. The funding provided financial support for my ambitions to teach people to sew, and very crucially, identify business partners who will hire them at living wages when they complete their training. "Fashion the Future Forward" is a first-of-its-kind effort to create space for women whose lives have been impacted by the criminal system through workforce training and a pathway to dignity through living-wage work in fashion. Grant Blvd's "Fashion the Future Forward" is an intensive training initiative designed to equip fellows with professional-level sewing skills in order to obtain employment in the home-goods and garment-production industries. Awareness of environmental impacts is foundational to our approach to education, design, and production. Fellows will commit to completing a six-week paid training program in order to be eligible for an eight-week paid internship in a Grant Blvd production facility. The goal of "Fashion the Future Forward" is to educate and empower women who will become permanent members of the Grant Blvd production staff, earning a living as creatives in an intentional community. Why? Because we need to completely reimagine our response to poverty and the criminalization of it, and we also have to radically change how we create pathways to self-sufficient living for Black and Brown people who've been incarcerated. This radical innovation in business design is about building radically inclusive pathways that pursue the long-term plan of progressing our collective good, and the good of our planet. It is a remarkable ambition and one of which I am incredibly proud.

I've learned that there's a fleeting moment of euphoria around "wins" like this. And I've also learned that they are often followed almost immediately by the panicked thought, "Now I have to do more work!" It falls on me to find a space, build a team, design a program, create employment channels, and construct careful systems for monitoring our impact.

People with secure, predictable jobs don't see the pressure you as a solo entrepreneur feel when you "win." Other people see it as shiny and bright, when you see it for what it is: a massive new undertaking. It's like being swept off your feet by an avalanche of pressure to deliver on what you thought you wanted and what you thought would be good for the business. Sometimes the wins add more pressure, but you need them to get to your goal.

If I had trained as an endurance athlete—a marathoner, an open-ocean swimmer—it would have been great preparation for raising capital. I wasn't an extreme athlete, but I did look back to see where I had endured. For me, it was the act of getting the Ph.D, of being able to see it through to the end when it took far longer and was more difficult than I had imagined. I reminded myself that I can go the distance when it really matters to me. My disrupted childhood and teenage traumas also showed me I can get through. Being married and going through a tumultuous divorce helped me to endure. If you look at your life, how you have stuck with it, army-crawled through obstacles, hung on when you could see absolutely nothing in front of you but darkness—seeing that about yourself can help you frame your chances for succeeding and maybe give you the faith that ultimately, you will succeed.

You might aspire to have a small business with a beautiful, niche vision, or you might aspire to build an empire. Both require your personal commitment over the long term. You have to make it through your first year, then press on to three years, then five, then ten, knowing no two of them will be the same. There is no "set it and forget it" about being an entrepreneur who wants to make their time count. I don't think you can definitively know how your investments of time, money, and energy in your business will play out. You certainly can't truly control timelines or outcomes.

But just because it is hard doesn't mean it can't be done. Which brings me to the next part of the social entrepreneur's journey: the care of your mental and emotional health.

## Key Takeaways:

- Confront your deepest feelings about money and debt. Separate what you were taught from what is actually true.

- Products and business "visions" do not attract investment capital. Investors invest in the daring leaders they believe in.

- Research a variety of funding options. Start with the lowest-risk option (probably crowdfunding) until you gain the knowledge to move up the investment ladder (loans might be next). Don't forget to evaluate your networks for those who might be able to support you by making warm introductions

- **For the vast majority of early-stage entrepreneurs, the need to fundraise never ends. This is especially true if you aspire to an aggressive vision.**

# CHAPTER TEN
## Preserving Your Body, Protecting Your Mind

Running a business of any size, but most especially a small, young business, means being surrounded on all sides by complex, often negative emotions. Grief, stress, anxiety, and what can feel like crippling isolation are an inescapable part of the landscape of your life as a leader. As a woman in business who is also a mother, I've also been forced to contend with shame, the threat of violence inside my shops, balancing multiple identities, navigating respectability politics, and managing the endless stress of making payroll. Caused by both the business and the busyness that being a CEO produces, these obstacles have at times triggered the wider, deeper emotions I've long carried with me. Simply put, being a CEO can be triggering.

What's more, if you expect and hope to have a life outside of your work as a business leader, that requires additional emotional energy. Women traditionally take on most of the caring and doing, only adding to the burden we have to hold as entrepreneurs. So most especially for women, there has to be a time to put this burden down and to step away from it. Part of my evolving awareness as a business leader showed me that the best way I could escape the weight of impending doom was to commit myself to exploring attainable ways to get relief.

## Surfing the Waves

I'm not a surfer, but I've learned a lot about being one because it's much like riding the uncertainties of business. From the time we begin planning our businesses, we position ourselves like the surfer on the shore, preparing mentally to pursue the great unknown beckoning us. It is an ocean of the unseen, powerful and vast in size. Like the surfer, we step tentatively into this cold, lonely environment, holding only the small piece of simple equipment (our boards) in pursuit of a wave we believe is going to find us. If we're lucky, we can manage that first wave, shakily figuring out our footing, catching the crest and riding it safely to shore as we planned. Encouraged by this first experience, we'll undoubtedly launch ourselves onto our boards again. Each success leads us to repeat the process over and over again. Until out of nowhere, something arises that has the power to sweep us away. That huge wave might be the consequence of something we did, or something we didn't know how to do. Sometimes too late, we realize we're going to crash—and hard. But we know this can't be the end. We take a moment to float, to catch our breath, to regain our strength, to reorient ourselves to the shore. Then, we make the choice to pull ourselves back on the board and to bravely go after that next big wave because we are simply, unshakably, not willing to quit. It's physically exhausting. It's emotionally taxing. It's creatively draining. The only way to survive is to rest in between waves. Without rest, the next challenge will wipe us out for good. The success we want rests in the ways we rest, the way we recover. The rest is where we win.

Even before I decided to launch Grant Blvd, I realized I had some deep personal work to do to level up. I knew I had to tap into and face what hurt so that I could stop running from it for good. This in itself was trying. It required both time and a financial commitment. But in going through an impossible divorce, I knew that I needed to be honest with myself. I needed to move on from a place where I made decisions because of my childhood traumas while refusing to see how those traumas were forcing their way to the surface through those choices. That realization led me to invest in therapeutic support, which I recognize as both a medical necessity and a privilege. That said, wellness, I'm convinced, is key to preparation for embracing change. Mentally and spiritually, I invested in personal growth. I found a therapist to help me make sense of my childhood of abandonment and to help me overcome being afraid, hurt, angry, alone, resentful, bitter, and anxious. That's a long list of deeply negative feelings and to be transparent, overcoming them took nine years of hard work in therapy with an amazing woman who changed my life. My therapist was a White woman who poured her rich blend of Buddhist philosophy, Irish heritage, and radical human empathy into me. Her caring support brought me to a place of radical acceptance. Instead of all the hurt, loss, and failure, she helped me see the humanity of my parents. And that open-heart acceptance did not just apply to my past life. She helped me carry that spirit into my present and future, and she stayed with me right up to her retirement, which coincided with my new beginning at Grant Blvd.

Therapy was another commitment I made. It was a long-term investment I made in myself. It has unarguably given me an incredible return for my efforts. And yet, none of this expression of radical compassion, acceptance, and kindness came easily or immediately to me. I had to develop an understanding of grace. I had to find language within myself to forgive my parents, to see them fully as people and not reductively as my parents. This commitment allowed me to forgive them before they asked for forgiveness—it allowed me to truly love them. Today, I'm in loving relationships with both of my parents because we each choose to accept that everyone's in their own fight and that each of us needs grace.

One brief aside: I've known many Black folk who are suspicious of White women and I know why they are distrustful (the history ain't no mystery). But, I don't hold on to a single story of White women, and I encourage anyone who feels that way to reconsider. I have been loved and championed by many, many incredible White women. They could see and make space for my experiences as a Black girl and later as a Black woman, and we've shared enduring bonds despite the walls that race in America create culturally. They became friends, sisters, and in some cases true mother figures. You can never tell where genuine love may come from, and I've found it can be a waste to let race be a barrier to receiving it.

No matter what claims the rich and famous make about themselves and their journeys, none of us ever reach our full potential alone. Some of us have parents or mentors or friends to guide us, or belief in a spiritual system that helps us make sense of the world and our role in it. For me, it was essential to find a third party I could trust, someone who gave me the space to disclose things that are hard to share, and who had the wisdom and expertise to help me come to terms with things that are impossible to forget. And it took a long journey of therapy to make sense of it all for me.

## Investing in Restoration

What shifted for me? In my thirties, I came to the decision that I wanted to be more judicious about using my money and time. I realized that I needed to invest in myself. I also came to see that I needed focused help. I was overwhelmed and confused, and I felt profoundly alone. What I couldn't have guessed was that this set of healing experiences gave me a toolbox of practices that I continue to come back to, even as my role and responsibilities in life have changed.

Actively engaging in therapy is an investment I would like you to consider if you haven't already. Realistically, I know this is asking a lot—financially, emotionally, and from a time perspective. I once felt that if I talked about the hardest things in my life, a huge dam would burst. I would cry so much I would somehow drown. I was terrified that if I opened up all the doors I thought I'd closed I'd never find my way back to my daily life. I'd forever be lost and trapped in an abyss of crippling sadness. But I can attest to the continued value of the practices it brought me to, practices I'd like to share with those of you who are on the front lines of disruption. Some of these healing methods require money, but all of them demand an even more precious resource: your time.

Being alone in nature restores me. I trace this back to my childhood jogs with my father in Milwaukee, but also to the time we spent in the parks, the woods and at the lakefront. Those early exposures still hold tremendous power for me. Even more now, as an adult with relentless responsibilities, I have come to rely on moments of solitude and silence as a way of recharging my energy and recalibrating my perspective. When I am alone in nature, be it in a public park, a private garden, or on a beach, I can reflect on the decisions I've made and their outcomes in ways I can't when I'm lost in the noise of the everyday. These moments of stillness don't require extensive or expensive travel. It might mean sitting in a meadow at dusk, finding a walking trail away from noisy roadways, or spreading a blanket on the banks of a lazy river or stream and simply watching the steady movement of the water—listening and breathing.

I have made regular pilgrimages to a place that makes immersion in nature and in my inner self possible. At Kripalu, a yoga retreat center in Massachusetts, I have been able to feed my soul by reading, jotting down my dreams, and making lists in ways that have been catalytic in both my growth as a business leader and in my personal journey. This process is also aided by my personal spiritual philosophy derived from a broad gamut of anchor texts: the Bible, contemporary thinkers like bell hooks and Marianne Williamson, as well as the poetry of David Whyte.

Another restorative tactic is simply the lost art of resting. The talk we all hear about "self-care" is mostly designed to sell us products. What I'm talking about is allowing yourself to experience genuine rest. Being still means stepping into a mental, emotional, physical space where you can see what is moving around you. One way I achieve this is through a daily morning practice of anchoring myself in my spiritual philosophy and journaling. I made this practice sacred, reserving for myself twenty minutes in the morning. My day begins when I set an intention for the tempo of the day. Focusing in a calm and clear manner lets me begin feeling less as if the day is running away from me—or running me—and more as if I have a deeper sense of relation with all that has to happen. I am recalibrating my relation to the work itself. I am choosing my adventure for the day.

My daily practice is a form of short-term rest, and something I have come to rely on. But these short bursts are not enough to sustain all the energy my business demands. Being still has to periodically be extended. My go-to method is a two-to-three-day getaway. Creating distance from my business, and even the day-to-day routine of my home, enables me to find perspective. I keep a journal while I'm taking a break because it helps me work out things that have happened and how I feel about them. It gives me the space to brainstorm what opportunities might come out of a crisis rather than being crushed by the crisis itself. Having the discipline to break away took me a long time to develop, but it can be cultivated. It's about discovering your relationship to a challenge and then reframing in your mind what is actually possible and when. I've learned that we can achieve a lot (and it's important to remain aware of where you are experiencing success), but we can't necessarily achieve everything at one time. This can be a painful reality when bills are due, but it can also be a tool for holding on to a healthy sense of perspective and protecting a positive outlook.

Less frequently than the brief breaks, you also have to remove yourself from everything you are managing for a longer stretch of time. This is crucial. I know how hard it is to step away for five to seven days when your business is anchored in you. It's hard to jump off a fast moving treadmill. But when I dedicate myself to the step away, I'm able to tap into my creativity in ways that only distance makes possible. I experience *novelty*, which is so important to the creative process. When we think about our businesses, we tend to fixate on operations, the ROI, our marketing efforts—all things we've talked about in this book. But moving into *execution* requires ideation for innovation. Whenever I travel—and again it doesn't have to be exotic or extravagant—I curate moments of learning. I see a wider world when I stand at new intersections. These longer trips can also allow for pouring more into relationships if you choose to travel with family members or friends. They are a way for us as business leaders to rediscover the other things we want to be tethered to and to rediscover our sense of choice. We need to feel like we are choosing our businesses; otherwise they become emotional and financial burdens that we secretly resent and loathe.

And on the topic of friends, let me say that they are the greatest antidote to the overwhelming loneliness felt by so many small-business owners. Another practice in protecting my peace has been building a robust network of colleagues in business, my friends and "co-conspirators," who understand how hard it is to be responsible for keeping a business afloat. Many of the folks in my community identify as Black or as women, and collectively they have given me a place to ideate, dream, and share my vision. But there are also thoughtful, tender men in this community who have the capacity to hold space for the realities of my experience. Community is key to winning in business. This group has helped its diverse members accomplish feats that we could never have pulled off on our own. We've used our resources to help score exposure on primetime TV, fundraise for each other, and we've encouraged each other. Even if you consider yourself an extreme introvert, please pour yourself into a local community of people who share your affinities. There is nothing like it. When you're holding your business in one hand and the narrative arc of your life in the other, it can feel like too much. If you have a group like mine, you can loosen your grip, set down the weight, and feel better.

The most effective rest schedule gives you different forms of relief. It's not all one thing only at certain times. The rest that feels best for you has to shift in response to what you're experiencing, what you can afford, and how much time you have to dedicate to preserving your own well-being. Putting a practice in place like this enables you to do the longer work of not just surviving in business but thriving in your fuller experience of being human. Stepping into stillness provides restoration—the energy to see what has to happen—and to do the work.

Surfers and waves, currents, stillness, and oceans of obligations. It's funny that water seems to be my go-to metaphorical medium. I didn't grow up near the ocean, but we did live close to Lake Michigan. People like me rarely step into the water there, where the shores were not welcoming to Black folks. My time in Milwaukee didn't give me much recreational exposure to water. Metaphorically, though, losing the security and comfort of my early years taught me how to find my way to shore. Those experiences helped me find the courage to put my toes in, walk up to my knees, and brace myself for the shock of diving in. I learned all this about surviving even though Grant Boulevard was seven miles from the lakeshore. My family home taught me how to be comfortable in rooms when I was the only person who looked like me, how to appreciate the world and cultures of the world, how to see and how to listen. Everything that came after taught me how to forgive and how to show up. Without doing that emotional work, without recognizing and honoring what we continue to need to live a full life, none of us is able to sustain our efforts to make change. So, let's think about what that change might be and how we swim toward it, even when the surf is cold, rough, and lonely. And no matter what, let's not forget: you're already in the water, which means, dear one, you're already on your way to meeting your full potential as an entrepreneur and business leader.

## Key Takeaways:

- **Being a woman business leader unleashes a tsunami of emotions, many of which are negative. Listen to the way you speak to yourself and protect yourself from toxic self-talk.**
- **Learn what feels healing to you and return to those healing places/practices regularly.**

- Rest is the best form of self-care. Learn what rest looks like for you.
- Friends, family, and your "found" community are held together with love (work) and forgiveness (grace). Love and grace will keep you striving, thriving, and living fully.

# CLOSING THOUGHTS:
# OPENING UP TO WHAT'S YET POSSIBLE

Not that long ago, we lived in an era of unions to protect the interests of American laborers and craftspeople. In the aftermath of the collapse of strong unions, it's now incumbent upon business leaders to stand in the gap. These laborers are our neighbors, spouses, sons and daughters, nieces and nephews. The business community has to think differently about how it is playing a part in stabilizing not just the economy but the future of our democracy. The challenge of this balancing act has to be taken up by business leaders globally, who must be made to acknowledge that our water belongs to all of us, our air is everyone's air. In short, our collective survival is dependent on collective action. That's not a lofty, deferred, long-term vision. This has to be addressed with a more intense sense of urgency and commitment than ever before in human history.

It's clear to me that many of us people feel, understandably, despondent and discouraged about the future of democracy and the fate of our planet. Challenging that narrative, offering a solution, being hopeful, and using business to contribute to the landscape of cities, including rural and suburban communities is how we have to right this ship. We can do that *and* pursue profit when we don't forget the importance of maintaining the balance of obligation we feel and not forgetting ourselves in the work.

My lofty, ambitious vision for the future of Grant Blvd is growing the business from a $3M valuation to a $30M valuation. I want us to be the go-to brand for global citizens who want their garments to reflect their commitment to protecting the planet's resources, while providing living-wage careers for textile workers. We want our logo to clearly state what and who we stand for. Through exceptional design, my companies aim to foster economic stability in communities across the country, offering and inspiring other workforce development opportunities in cities where the poverty and crime rates are degrading the quality of life for all of us. And someday, I hope to see my daughter take over as creative director.

What we've pioneered at Grant Blvd is an example of how more businesses can and should create a culture of care. It is past time for our business and political leaders to figure out how to return domestic manufacturing and living-wage jobs to America. We should all be thinking about our government and businesses and how they promote equity through their policies and products. How mindful they are of the planet. Traditionally, we have ignored those aspects in our endless quest for the best goods at the cheapest price.

As you work on gaining influence, building social-impact businesses, and creating impact, you will constantly be asked how you measure success. We must begin by acknowledging that the traditional metrics for success are purely financial, derived from a colonialist, exploitative business model. A bulging, ever-expanding "healthy" bottom line does not take into account the costs paid by workers, communities, natural resources, or the planet. When you care for and support all of these other concerns, profits will suffer. But isn't that preferable to human suffering and environmental disaster?

What are the impacts and outcomes you want your business to achieve? How will you communicate these in compelling ways to gain and retain the support your business will always need? I believe we begin by redefining and then modeling what it means to be a daring leader. We conduct our businesses in ways that treat people with respect, avoid contributing to climate catastrophe, and strive to overthrow the exploitative approach of colonialism. It is critical that we measure our own successes by this different set of standards. Because we are pioneers and social entrepreneurism remains a frontier, we have to be patient with ourselves. It's important to realize that your experiments and innovations may not work out as you hoped, or that the desired outcomes may prove slow in appearing. Are your employees happy and fulfilled in their workplace? Does your business promote and contribute to building a strong, diverse, resilient community? Does your customer base represent the rich fabric that is America? Other people may not see these milestones as worthy of reward, but they are a sign that you are doing something remarkable. If you can see these traits in your business, surely you are helping to build a business community that is a positive force for a better future for all. This must be at the center of the future of capitalism.

There are no Olympic medals awaiting us for what we are striving to do, and yet the odds are as long as those facing aspiring Olympians. This is really, really hard work. Like superior athletes, we have to learn to push through the pain and to always do our best. Unlike those athletes, we'll never stand on the podium to have a medal hung around our necks. Our rewards will have to come from our employees, our customers, our communities, and very importantly, from ourselves, recognizing that we have gone against the norm to use our time on earth to accomplish something better than a swollen bank account.

Millions of entrepreneurs, creatives, and corporate decision-makers are rising up, recognizing the power of the business sector to create positive change, and discovering an inescapable sense of urgency. We come from tales of other shorelines and other journeys. Our great work is to share our stories and our journey in the service of other people and this our one precious planet. Globally, businesses can thrive and be profitable while making ethical decisions about what's in the best interest of *all* people.

My vision for the corporations I build and lead are that they become agents of change and living examples of what is yet still possible. This is what I hope for you as a leader, too. My other hope, my other true aspiration, is that your approach to design and leadership will become a beacon of light wherever it exists. That you as a daring business leader, will become another guiding star. I believe that all of this is possible as long as we each practice endurance and protect our optimism. May we each always protect our biggest dreams and dare to build it boldly.

*Kimberly*
DR. MCGLONN

www.drkimberlymcglonn.com
IG: @kimberlymcglonn
IG: @grantblvd

# ABOUT THE AUTHOR

Dr. Kimberly McGlonn's life is a story of two childhoods and two Americas. Born on the North Side of Milwaukee, a city Dr. Martin Luther King once called the "Selma of the North," she was afforded all the comforts of middle-class life. However, when McGlonn was twelve, all that changed. What came next taught her about the consequences and shame of poverty, the pathways that can lead to incarceration, and the obstacles poor women must navigate. These lessons shape her views on not just the global economy, but the way forward for the common good in America. Here, she calls on the world's 524 million entrepreneurs to embrace a new kind of activism and legacy-building, one that puts people and the planet in the balance of the pursuit of profit, challenges systemic racism, and protects us from the worst of the climate catastrophe. She offers sage wisdom on what daring leadership requires and how we can use business design to create powerful impacts.

# Enjoyed Reading
## *Build It Boldly?*

## "The best way to thank an author is to leave a review!"

Want to show your support of this new approach to business design and to help inspire others? Please find *Build It Boldly* on Amazon or your preferred platform for finding new books and leave a review! This one, simple action will help us lead the leaders of tomorrow as they #builditboldly.

## Ready to take the lessons of *Build It Boldly* to the next level?

*Build It Boldly* courses are available online now!
Visit www.builditboldly.com

Use code BIB50 for $50 off any course!

www.ingramcontent.com/pod-product-compliance
Lightning Source LLC
Chambersburg PA
CBHW071418210326
41597CB00020B/3561